"The siren call of self sings loudly i[n]
as Christians, we easily fall prey to
care, and self-love. With a refresh
and insight, Lydia Brownback invites us to consider our ways with
fruitful reflection. *Flourish* is a book every woman should read. I highly
recommend it!"

Melissa Kruger, author, *In All Things* and *The Envy of Eve*

"As someone who deals in words all day and every day, I'm always
fascinated to see how they come and go, how they ebb and flow.
Recent years have brought us countless articles, books, podcasts,
and conferences based on the word *flourish*. 'Follow this program,'
they say, or 'switch to this diet,' or 'become more mindful,' and 'you'll
finally flourish in your life and in your relationships. Guaranteed!' In
this book, Lydia Brownback looks for and finds what I'm convinced
is the true key to human flourishing. Her solution is infinitely better because it is based on an infinitely better source—the enduring,
infallible Word of God."

Tim Challies, blogger, *Challies.com*

"Lydia Brownback is an author to be trusted. She writes with lucid insight and biblical discernment. The result is a book that is truly helpful—
a book that avoids contemporary fads and points the reader repeatedly
to the sufficiency of Christ. She takes on common destructive states of
mind that often hinder Christians from walking in the freedom that is
theirs by grace. I suppose the highest recommendation I can give to
this book is that it is one I will be encouraging the congregation I serve
to read."

Todd Pruitt, Lead Pastor, Covenant Presbyterian Church,
Harrisonburg, Virginia; Cohost, *Mortification of Spin*

"What if the pathway to true flourishing is not what our instincts assume? What if the siren calls of society and culture are misleading us? What if real flourishing makes foolish the wisdom of the world and turns today's prevailing solution on its head? What if self-focus leads to losing the life that really matters, and focusing outside ourselves leads to finding it? Lydia Brownback has a beat on the answer. There is a true flourishing, and it may not be what you think—and it is better than what we dream. This is no shallow guide to 'flourishing' when all in life is well. Brownback wants to get us ready to truly flourish—when all around our soul gives way."

David Mathis, Executive Editor, desiringGod.org; Pastor, Cities Church, Minneapolis/St. Paul, Minnesota; author, *Habits of Grace*

"In a world where seemingly every voice whispers, 'Think about yourself,' this book is an invitation to something better. With biblical clarity, Lydia Brownback exposes the pervasive lie of self-focus and points us to a more abundant life. Whether you find yourself shackled to the self-centered spirit of the age or mentoring someone else who is, *Flourish* will open the prison door and let in the warm light of Christ."

Megan Hill, author, *Contentment* and *Praying Together*; Editor, The Gospel Coalition

Flourish

Other Crossway Books by Lydia Brownback

Contentment: A Godly Woman's Adornment

Finding God in My Loneliness

Joy: A Godly Woman's Adornment

Purity: A Godly Woman's Adornment

Sing a New Song: A Woman's Guide to the Psalms

Trust: A Godly Woman's Adornment

A Woman's Wisdom: How the Book of Proverbs Speaks to Everything

Flourish

*How the Love of Christ
Frees Us from Self-Focus*

Lydia Brownback

WHEATON, ILLINOIS

Trade paperback ISBN: 978-1-4335-6065-1
ePub ISBN: 978-1-4335-6068-2
PDF ISBN: 978-1-4335-6066-8
Mobipocket ISBN: 978-1-4335-6067-5

Library of Congress Cataloging-in-Publication Data

Names: Brownback, Lydia, 1963– author.
Title: Flourish : how the love of Christ frees us from self-focus / Lydia Brownback.
Description: Wheaton : Crossway, 2019. | Includes bibliographical references and index.
Identifiers: LCCN 2018026104 (print) | LCCN 2018044341 (ebook) | ISBN 9781433560668 (pdf) | ISBN 9781433560675 (mobi) | ISBN 9781433560682 (epub) | ISBN 9781433560651 (tp)
Subjects: LCSH: Christian women—Religious life.
Classification: LCC BV4527 (ebook) | LCC BV4527 .B7653 2019 (print) | DDC 248.8/43—dc23
LC record available at https://lccn.loc.gov/2018026104

Crossway is a publishing ministry of Good News Publishers.

LB		29	28	27	26	25	24	23	22	21	20	19
15	14	13	12	11	10	9	8	7	6	5	4	3	2

With gratitude to God
for
Jessie Joy Bible Yang
1969–2018
You marked my life indelibly.
And, selfishly, I wish you hadn't left so soon.

Contents

Introduction

What's trending? Tracking trends—in fashion, food, and everything else—is a hobby for some and a full-time career for others. Even those of us who care little about keeping up with trends are still curious as to what's hot and what's not. What's the fascination? Trends are a big deal because they tap into our thirst for the new and novel. In reality though, there's nothing new under the sun (Eccles. 1:9), so all trends are simply the repackaging of something old.

Cultural icons aren't the only fodder for trendsetters. It happens with ideas and beliefs as well. Even particular words rise and fall in popularity. As I write, the word *flourish* is having a moment. It's a good trend, this word *flourish*, because it conveys what life in Christ is meant to be—enjoying the Lord and living for him. It's about serving with gladness, not drudgery. It's getting beyond the ho-hum, going-through-motions sort of Christian living and knowing Christ as our greatest delight.

We want that, right? And not just the occasional flash of it, but all the time. We want a flourishing lifestyle. So why don't we have it? What's in the way? What sabotages our joy?

For most of us, it's nothing big and dramatic; it's the little daily pressures—the stresses and fears and irritations—that come along and disrupt our intentions to live and love well. But there's often more to it. Humdrum joylessness comes also from what we take into our hearts and minds not only from the world around us but from sources that claim to be Christian. That's what we want to make sense of as we make our way through this book. We want to see how wrong teaching about God can give us wrong ideas about God and how these wrong ideas keep us from flourishing.

To ground ourselves, it's important to realize that we are living in the time the Bible calls "the last days." When Jesus returned to his Father in heaven forty days after his resurrection, this new era of history began—the last days—and we're told by God's Word that this era will be characterized by trouble. It's a sobering truth, but the apostle Paul wants us to face this reality head on: "Understand this," he wrote to Timothy, "in the last days there will come times of difficulty" (2 Tim. 3:1). And then he explains why these days will be so hard:

> People will be lovers of self, lovers of money, proud, arrogant, abusive, disobedient to their parents, ungrateful, unholy, heartless, unappeasable, slanderous, without self-control, brutal, not loving good, treacherous, reckless, swollen with conceit, lovers of pleasure rather than lovers of God, having the appearance of godliness, but denying its power. Avoid such people. (vv. 2–5)

As you look at Paul's list of difficulties, do you see the repeated word? It's *love*—more specifically, misplaced love. Times of difficulty arise because people are lovers of themselves and lovers of money and lovers of pleasure rather than lovers of good and lovers of God.

So many of the scary, evil things we see happening arise from the poison of misplaced love, and as Paul says earlier in this letter, it's "spread like gangrene" by false teachers (2 Tim. 2:17).

Paul is saying that people are spiritually poisoned when they drink in wrong teaching about God's Word and God's ways, and that's why he tells us to avoid it—to keep ourselves away from wrong teaching. There's simply no escaping the fact that we're always conformed to what we focus on.

If we want to know joy and peace, if we desire to be fruitful disciples of the Lord Jesus, it's imperative that we breathe the right spiritual air. But how do we know what that is? How can we be sure that we're taking in air that's spiritually healthy?

Our challenge is to discern teaching that's pure and true from that which is toxic and false. God's Word is our standard, of course. But here's the tricky part: wrong teaching about the Bible can significantly shape the way we understand the Bible! That's why it's vital to be able to identify what's false—in other words, unbiblical—in the materials we allow into our eyes and ears. So our approach seems pretty straightforward—safeguard ourselves in biblical truth—but it's actually more challenging than we realize. We need to take a closer look. As we do, we're likely to discover that we've unwittingly bought into some of this false teaching because it's been presented to us as truth.

The whole idea of "false teaching" brings to mind images of slick televangelists or cultlike groups living on the fringe. But look again at Paul's words to Timothy and notice the very first thing he mentions about the last days: "People will be lovers of self." Any teaching that sets self-love as the highest good is false teaching, and we are susceptible to it because it appeals to that deep yearning for affirmation we feel at our very core. That's why it hooks us. It just *feels* so right. And there is an inescapable link between self-love and self-focus. Self-love and self-focus are really just flipsides of the same coin. They always go together. That's why self-love, the sort that the apostle was writing about, directs our energies, thoughts, plans, choices—and even our theology—inward, making ourselves the center of all things.

Are we self-lovers of this sort? We might be—if we define ourselves by what people think of us. We might be—if we believe that walking with Jesus is all about maximizing our personal potential. We might be—if we allow our feelings to govern our choices. We might be—if we think Jesus saved us primarily to make our daily life more comfortable. We might be—if we allow some sin, whether past or present, to define us. Fixating on ourselves never accomplishes what we hope it will, so we need to let go of it and fixate on someone else—the Lord Jesus Christ. God's Word—and true biblical teaching—is all about him.

So take a moment to scan the pile of books on your nightstand, specifically those that have to do with the Christian faith. Is there a common theme among those titles? How many have more to do with successful Christian living than with Christ himself? While Christian-living books can certainly be good and helpful, they can actually warp our understanding of what it means to be a Christian if Christ isn't at the center of them. So we want to be wise and discerning not only in our book choices but also in every form of teaching we imbibe, from preaching to podcasts.

We've got our work cut out for us.

But as we become biblically equipped to distinguish between self-love and Christ-love, our walk of faith will flourish, and we'll find the abundant life Jesus promised.

Set Free from Self-Consciousness

A few years ago, selfie sticks hit the market. They were the "it" Christmas gift that year for the under-thirty set (and many over thirty, as well). In fact, the selfie stick was listed in *Time* magazine's twenty-five best inventions of 2014. Nothing better captures the spirit of our era than this extendable metal rod that enables people to position a camera for the taking of endless self-portraits. Some have dubbed it the "Wand of Narcissus." And for good reason.

Selfies fuel the engine of social media. Many of us change our profile pictures weekly or even daily. Some of these are candid, in-the-moment, fun shots, but many are the result of countless takes and retakes, angling for that perfect one that sets us off to best advantage. The age of the selfie (and the fact that selfies are even a *thing*) allows us to influence how others answer the question we are always asking ourselves: "What do people think of *me*?"

By means of our clothes, our weight, our gym routine, the interior of our home, the behavior of our children, and even how we birth our children, we are so easily driven by a craving for an acceptable answer to that question. But in Christ, we are called to ask a different question: What do people think of Christ? When we are driven by a concern for how people perceive him, we can live free from the bondage of what people think of us. One of the most amazing aspects of being united to Christ by faith is that he actually becomes our very identity, but not until we grasp this truth can we enjoy the freedom of self-forgetfulness.

Dig

Freedom is the best gift a democracy offers its citizens. Those of us who have lived our whole lives under a democratic system tend to take freedom for granted. We aren't typically filled with wonder that we are free to choose a career path, whom to marry, the size of our family, and where (and whom) to worship. But these freedoms we enjoy were hard-won, handed down to us through risk and bloodshed and wars. Our national history, however, is merely a short-lived shadow of the eternal freedom Jesus won for us when he shed his blood on the cross to free us from sin and God's wrath. When Jesus rose from the dead and ascended back to heaven, he actually took us with him:

> But God, being rich in mercy, because of the great love with which he loved us, even when we were dead in our trespasses, made us alive together with Christ—by grace you have been saved—and raised us up with him and seated us with him in the heavenly places in Christ Jesus. (Eph. 2:4–6)

Our life is now there, in the heavenly places with Christ. This isn't just some spiritual concept to ponder; it's a reality with enormous practical implications. For our purposes here, it indicates that Jesus won for us freedom from ourselves. We can take our society's freedoms for granted and still enjoy those benefits, but not so much our spiritual freedom. If we take for granted Christ's work for us, or if we don't understand all he has done, we live and think like prisoners rather than free women.

I think, for example, of Sophia. Each weekday she arises at six o'clock and spends fifteen minutes sipping coffee and doing her daily Bible reading. Afterward she turns her attention to the day ahead, and she thinks about what to wear as she finishes her coffee. Thoughts of God and the Bible passage she's just read fade from her mind as she stares at the clothes rack. Sophia is focused on the image she wants to project and how her clothing choice will be viewed by the people she'll encounter in the hours ahead. Once dressed, accessorized, and made up, she heads downstairs for breakfast, and while she scrambles eggs for the family, she ponders whether she can afford the calories if she partakes. There's that dress she's got to fit into for the reunion next month, so maybe she'll just skip the toast. And on it goes throughout the day, right up through bedtime.

But even bedtime doesn't free Sophia from self-consciousness. The busyness of the day might be over, but these quieter moments allow her the mental space to scan back through the day's activities and conversations for the impressions she made. Things she said or didn't say or wish she'd said or should have said or rephrased—it's all there once her head hits the pillow.

Sophia doesn't see the bondage in which she's living, but her anxieties about her appearance and her words reveal it. Sophia is so focused on herself, curved so entirely inward, that she is locked in a self-made prison. That's what self-consciousness is—a prison.

If we center our thoughts and activities on ourselves, our world grows increasingly narrow, and over time our view of reality is warped. Without realizing it, we become the measure of all things in our own minds.

"What Will People Think of Me?"

Self-consciousness impacts the decisions we make. Our choices big and small are too often governed by *What will people think of me?* Our attempt to shape the answer to that question can become an internal undercurrent so relentless that we aren't even aware of its pull. It can be there in the home furnishings we choose. It can be there in the tables we set and the planter we place on the patio. It can be there in the car we drive and the holiday decorations we choose for the front porch. And it can be there in the books we read and the restaurants we frequent and the places we choose for vacation.

Self-consciousness can also drive the decisions we make for our children. The schools they attend and the summer camps, the clothes they wear and the friends they bring home—that relentless undercurrent might be flowing somewhere beneath our very genuine mama-bear love. Angry words, shame, and impatience so easily arise from *What will people think of me?*

It can begin even before our children are born. As the baby grows within us, we seek advice and do research on how to be the best possible mom. We note what other mothers do and how they do it, setting standards for our mothering techniques along the way. We distinguish not only good from bad, but best from better. Sometimes, though, we wind up not only wanting to be the ideal mom but yearning to be *known* as that mom.

One young mother was devastated when her plans for natural, at-home childbirth could not be realized. Complications during the final weeks of pregnancy necessitated a hospital delivery. Two years later she continues to agonize. She views herself as a failure for not giving birth the way she'd envisioned. She can't see that she didn't fail her child, who was born healthy and continues to thrive. And she didn't fail her Lord, who nowhere in Scripture mandates a particular method of childbirth. She failed only herself in not living up to what had become standard practice among the young mothers in her circle.

When it comes to self-conscious motherhood, the method and the means of childbirth are just the beginning. There's also the pressure to make baby food from scratch and to use only cloth diapers. Love drives many moms to make these choices, but there are equally as many who make them because they seem to fit an ideal-mother identity. These moms can't see that they are driven more by self-induced standards than by love, and in time all the joy leaches out of their mothering.

If we are self-conscious mothers, that undercurrent will continue to tug at us when it comes time to make decisions about schooling our children. Certainly we set out to make informed, careful choices about where and how to educate our kids, and those choices are likely to vary from child to child. As we research schooling prospects, we wisely gather opinions from more experienced parents, but what matters here is their view on education, not their view of us. I've known more than one depressed and angry homeschooling mother whose dark emotions had less to do with a sense of inadequacy or burnout than with the initial reason for homeschooling—the perceived expectations of others. No doubt these moms chose homeschooling because they wanted the best for their kids, but other good (perhaps better) options for their particular family were pulled down in the undertow of *What will people think?*

Discern

Whatever the issue—our appearance, our family, our home, our kids—we quench the joy of our faith and mar our witness of Christ if we live self-conscious lives. It seems counterintuitive, but happiness comes not from being thought well of but by thinking less of ourselves altogether.

Body and Soul

Not all of us have children to raise or homes to furnish, but we all have bodies to present to the world on a daily basis. Living, as we do, in a society where youth and muscle tone are icons of success, the temptation to measure up can be enormous. We are well aware of the pressures put on women by society, and those of us who know God's Word seek to combat them by regularly cultivating an eternal perspective. We turn to verses such as 1 Timothy 4:8, where Paul writes, "While bodily training is of some value, godliness is of value in every way." Even so, we may find ourselves giving too much thought and too many dollars and too much time to how we look.

I grew up on the tail end of that first skinny-obsessed generation. Twiggy came along in the 1960s, effectually abolishing the Marilyn Monroe hourglass ideal, and eventually the Twiggy trend led to full-fledged emaciated heroin chic in the 1990s. Girls in my generation got hooked by all this, and many of us have never become unhooked. Additionally, significant scientific developments during these decades opened our eyes to the health dangers of a high-fat diet, obesity, and a sedentary lifestyle. To this day we are tempted to define our well-being by our body weight. And adopting the cultural standard, we use *thin* and *toned* as synonyms for *successful* and *godly*.

Even so, worldly influence isn't our only challenge to a right understanding of biblical discipleship. Equally influential is how that worldly influence has infiltrated our churches. Common on many a church's activities list today are exercise classes with names like "Body and Soul Fitness." These are basically the same fitness programs offered at any gym, but they are rebranded as Christian by contemporary praise music and an emphasis on good health for the glory of God. It all sounds great. Exercise is indeed valuable, as Paul said, and we do bring glory to God by taking care of our physical bodies. And how better to do so than in company with other believers all spinning and stretching to praise tunes?

But there's a bit more to consider. First is the context of Paul's words about exercise:

> Have nothing to do with irreverent, silly myths. Rather train yourself for godliness; for while bodily training is of some value, godliness is of value in every way, as it holds promise for the present life and also for the life to come. (1 Tim. 4:7–8)

What sticks in our minds is the middle of this passage—"bodily training is of some value." We see it as biblical endorsement for regular workouts. But Paul's point here is something quite different. He was trying to clear up confusion caused by false teachers about the nature of true godliness. Believers in his day were wrestling with false teaching that equated strict self-denial—also called "asceticism"—with godliness. In other words, self-denial and suppressing bodily appetites were supposedly a mark of true godliness. So Paul here is instructing Timothy to counter that lie with the truth that strict bodily discipline and godliness don't necessarily go hand in hand. Exercise is good and godliness is good, but they aren't bound up together. In fact, only one is a necessity, spiritually speaking.

The majority of these "Body and Soul" classes have no intention of promoting the heresy of Paul's day; even so, they can create an environment that is conducive to drifting that way. Another potential danger of such classes is how they can impact our view of God's Word. Choreographing exercise classes to Scripture passages can unwittingly trivialize God's Word, and our understanding of biblical discipleship can become warped.

In a different epistle Paul *does* set forth the merits of bodily discipline (see 1 Cor. 9:27). Even so, from the number of godly saints who suffer serious illnesses—both those who exercise and those who don't—it seems that God's concern for the shape and even the health of our bodies is radically different from ours.

Certainly it is God glorifying to take care of the body God has entrusted to us, but some of these exercise classes do little more than place a spiritual veneer over our efforts to feel good about ourselves. If we participate in this sort of exercise program, let's think about how we are being affected by it. Are we fired up at the end of class, awash in the sweaty glow of an endorphin high, to run out and evangelize or race home to read Scripture and pray? Perhaps, but more likely, we simply bask in how good we feel and get on with our day. And while that good feeling is a blessing, sometimes it's there because the workout has provided us a quick fix for the next time we're assailed by the relentless question, *What will people think of me?*

Exercise classes are the drug of choice for many a self-consciousness junkie. And the remedy for many of them isn't to stop asking the question—*What will people think of me?*—but simply to shape how it's answered.

Perception Management

Another popular attempt to remedy the anxiety of self-consciousness lies in the opposite direction. Rather than winning people's approval, we try to elevate ourselves above caring what others think of us. But contrary to popular teaching, this is no remedy; it's simply self-consciousness hiding behind a defensive shield.

Scan some popular websites, and you'll find endless how-tos for perception management, cultivating self-love, and engaging in positive self-talk, many of them directed at teens. What are we imbibing, and what message are we instilling in our daughters? And how much of either is rooted in Scripture? We cannot assume that material labeled "Christian" is actually biblical, but discerning truth from error is a challenge, especially when truth is mixed with error. A well-meaning author, seeking to encourage girls who struggle with a low self-opinion, guides her readers to think of themselves in light of who Jesus is:

> This is who I am:
>
> I am a sinner—elaborately flawed by my own self. I screw up consistently, so much so that some days I don't even realize how much I have sinned.
>
> But I am saved and forgiven and enough. I am worthy and valuable and significant—not because of anything I did, but because Jesus has deemed me His.[1]

Good stuff there, which the author draws from Genesis 1:31: "God saw everything that he had made, and behold, it was very good." The mistake she makes is building her advice on this alone, leaving out the Bible's overarching storyline. As a result, her encouraging words actually lead her readers away from truth, which is clear from what she writes next:

> Sometimes I like to dream about what the world would look like if we all chose to believe that how God made us is entirely good enough. And then I go one step further and start to dream about what the world would look like if we not only

believed we were enough, but believed that who we are is just plain good.[2]

The big picture of the Bible shows us that God's good creation was marred when sin entered the world. From that point on, every person is, from birth, just like the apostle Paul, who wrote, "I know that nothing good dwells in me, that is, in my flesh" (Rom. 7:18). God did indeed make us "very good," but if this is all that readers are given, they won't find the help and hope they need.

I get what the author is trying to do here and that she means well, but we have to be careful of any teaching, no matter how small a portion, that runs counter to something in Scripture. The young women who read the article are left believing that salvation makes *them* good rather than that salvation is how *Christ's* goodness is given to them. Truth plus error does not equal partial truth; truth plus error equals error.

We cannot overcome self-consciousness by trying to become all we can be or by telling ourselves we are good. We overcome it by seeing the sin that underlies it, the *me* focus.

Flourish

The problem with self-consciousness isn't the emotional angst it produces or caring too much what others think of us. The problem is thinking too much about ourselves—period. Living in the freedom of self-forgetfulness begins with discernment. We begin by making a link between our self-conscious tendencies and what we are drinking in not only from our culture but also from teaching that misapplies God's Word to our day-in, day-out life. And we acknowledge that, ultimately, those influences capture us because our heart resonates with what they're pitching: personal well-being, success, and our neighbors' admiration. Our self-consciousness is proof that we crave those things. God's Word clearly indicates that self-consciousness is bondage:

> The fear of man lays a snare,
>> but whoever trusts in the LORD is safe. (Prov. 29:25)

This proverb is addressed to people pleasers, to those who seek their well-being in the good opinion of others. But looking for well-being in people's opinions dislodges God from his rightful place in our hearts. He is the one we've been created to please.

Overcoming the Fear of Man

Ultimately, fear of man is a craving to please ourselves; we want people to admire us so we can feel valuable and important. But God is the One whose value and importance we are called to showcase. So the proverb sheds light on the people-pleasing problem. But it also shows us the path out. It is trust in the Lord that frees us from the snare of self-consciousness. If we shift our gaze away from ourselves and up to the Lord, we find that he is trustworthy and faithful to be all he has promised to be and to do all he has promised to do.

Something amazing happens as our trust grows: our thoughts are a lot less self-oriented, and there's new joy in living. We taste the freedom that comes from living under the gaze of One. He loves us, and we have nothing to prove because Christ proved everything for us.

As we trust, our focus on people changes too. We stop viewing others as a measure of ourselves but as people to love. We stop using them and begin serving them. We *are* meant to focus on others, just not with ourselves as the reference point. These are the blessings of self-forgetfulness. A young woman named Ava modeled this for me.

I first met Ava about a decade ago at a church retreat for high school girls. She was a bit more reserved than some of her classmates but warm and friendly nevertheless. She was also one of the most naturally beautiful sixteen-year-olds I had ever seen. And she had a heart for God. That weekend began a friendship that lasted through Ava's college years. She suffered some painful circumstances during those years, but with each challenge, she sought to know the Lord better and serve him more faithfully. Ava and I lost touch after she graduated from college, but just recently she wrote me a note, and we arranged to meet at a local café. I was a bit nervous as I drove to meet her because the picture that had accompanied her note to me clearly indicated another challenge—she was completely bald. Her note had included no explanation for the baldness. Was it some new form of millennial chic, or did she have cancer?

When I arrived at the café, Ava was already there, and as she came toward me, it wasn't her bald head I noticed nearly so much as that lovely Ava smile, still the most eye-catching aspect of her person. Turns out she doesn't have cancer. Nor was she making a fashion statement. She has alopecia, a condition that brings about hair loss—in some cases, such as Ava's, total loss. "It's only hair," she said, "and the important thing is, I'm healthy." She went on to tell me how God has used this to deepen her faith and her commitment to serve him, and she talked joyfully about all the ways that's been happening. Ava's trust is deep—and she is utterly unself-conscious.

On the way home from our meeting, I wept, but not for Ava. I wept for how an hour in her company had exposed my sinful self-consciousness. I recalled how I'd panicked during a season of middle-aged hair thinning a few years back. I'd cried. I'd prayed. I'd rushed to the dermatologist. I'd obsessed—all because my formerly thick hair had become a bit less thick. I continued to weep as I recalled the disappointment over the years on faces of friends whose homemade goodies I'd declined out of concerns rooted in vanity. I wept for the hours (days, weeks, months) lost to fixating on myself rather than on things that really matter—love for the Lord and for people. For years I'd mentored Ava, and that day she unknowingly mentored me.

Like Ava, the apostle Paul, one of most joyful people ever to walk this earth, lived free from the snare of self-consciousness. He didn't worry what people said or thought about him. Paul's focus was what people thought of Christ:

> I, when I came to you, brothers, did not come proclaiming to you the testimony of God with lofty speech or wisdom. For I decided to know nothing among you except Jesus Christ and him crucified. And I was with you in weakness and in fear and much trembling, and my speech and my message were not in plausible words of wisdom, but in demonstration of the Spirit and of power, so that your faith might not rest in the wisdom of men but in the power of God. (1 Cor. 2:1–5)

Jesus was Paul's whole reason for living, and because that was true, he saw his personal weaknesses as opportunities to show God's strength.

Jesus Christ was also Paul's whole *identity*, which he affirms in his letter to the Galatians:

> I have been crucified with Christ. It is no longer I who live, but Christ who lives in me. And the life I now live in the flesh I live by faith in the Son of God, who loved me and gave himself for me. (Gal. 2:20)

Paul defined himself by his union with Christ, not by the opinions of others or by ministry success or by personal characteristics or achievements. His Christ identity set him free from the life-leaching bondage of sinful self-consciousness and enabled him to practice what he preached: "Indeed, I count everything as loss because of the surpassing worth of knowing Christ Jesus my Lord. For his sake I have suffered the loss of all things and count them as rubbish, in order that I may gain Christ" (Phil. 3:8).

Christ is our identity too, if we've been united to him by faith. Sometimes we forget that. Some of us have never understood it. And it gets obscured by our naturally self-oriented hearts. Focusing upward and outward transforms us into women characterized by what Tim Keller calls "gospel-humility":

> The essence of gospel-humility is not thinking more of myself or thinking less of myself, it is thinking of myself less. Gospel-humility is not needing to think about myself.... True gospel-humility means I stop connecting every experience, every conversation, with myself. In fact, I stop thinking about myself.[3]

Christ defines us, not other people. And what he thinks is all that really matters.

> I tell you, my friends, do not fear those who kill the body, and after that have nothing more that they can do. But I will warn you whom to fear: fear him who, after he has killed, has authority to cast into hell. Yes, I tell you, fear him! Are not five sparrows sold for two pennies? And not one of them is forgotten before God. Why, even the hairs of your head are all numbered. Fear not; you are of more value than many sparrows. (Luke 12:4–7)

Set Free from Self-Improvement

Are you a list person? If so, you understand people like me, who anchor every day with a list. Each morning I set out my to-dos, and as the day wears on, I check off each thing as it gets done. There's something so satisfying about it, especially those days when every item gets crossed off by bedtime. And those of us blessed with smartphones can go nuts with the notes feature, working off several lists at any one time. I've got the chore list; the one for ministry outreach; another for Bible studies and writing projects; and yet another for more long-range plans.

Even if we aren't list people, every one of us is goal-oriented. Big or small, we set goals, and we strive to reach them every day. Two things about goal setting are helpful to think about: the *what* and the *why*.

If you think back over your goals for the last month, can you see a common theme? Identifying a theme is a way of getting at the *what*—not each individual goal so much, but what ties all those individual goals together. Is there some aspect that unifies them—a commonality? Maybe it's family. Or maybe it's something to do with your job or your spiritual walk.

And then the *why*—why do we strive to reach goals? Why do they matter to us?

My friend Zoe's goal is to declutter her house. Truth be told, it *is* cluttered, and I don't mean a few piles here and there. Zoe collects things—furniture, knickknacks, dishes—and the collections take up tables and counter space and a lot of the floor. All the clutter prevents her from inviting people over—something she says she'd love to do. Decluttering has been Zoe's goal ever since I've known her, and I've known her for twenty-plus years. Every so often she'll set aside a day to tackle it, but I've never seen any real progress.

Recently I asked her how Jesus factors into her decluttering goal, and she told me she's never really thought about that. The goal's always been sufficiently in the background of her life, a sort of white noise, but as we talked, she said she was going to start praying for God's help to achieve it. "He'll help me," she said, "because I know he wants me to feel good about myself."

Then there's Hayley, another woman who hesitates to host friends, but clutter isn't her problem. In Hayley's case, it's fear of not measuring up. Most of her friends have nicer furnishings, and they seem to host with such confidence.

Hayley's aware that her fear is really pride, and it stands in the way of doing any kind of loving hospitality. So her inability to master this sin leaves her frustrated and discouraged and ashamed. And she finds herself wondering, "Why won't God help me?"

We all know women like Zoe and Hayley, and very likely, we can see one or both of them reflected in how we deal with the various things we don't like about ourselves or how we handle our lives. So when it comes to personal goal setting, it's worth pondering again the apostle Paul's words: "Whether you eat or drink, *or whatever you do*, do all to the glory of God" (1 Cor. 10:31).

When we consider Zoe in light of Paul's instruction, I think it's safe to say that God *would* delight to help her declutter—not because clutter robs him of glory, but because clutter inhibits hospitality. As for Hayley, the problem isn't her décor, but the fact that her thoughts are consumed by it.

The same principle applies when it comes to all our personal goals. Are we pursuing personal change in order to enrich our walk with God and to shine better light on the gospel, or are we basically just dissatisfied with ourselves? And a related question to ponder: Do we hate sin because it's sin or because of the painful consequences it brings?

Dig

As we examine our motivations for change, let's start by thinking about why, hard as we try, some of our goals never get reached.

In Zoe's case, she doesn't realize that anxiety underlies her failure. It's hard to pinpoint, but here it is: if she finally got her house in order, she'd lose a vital component of what enables her to keep focused on herself. She'd feel a bit empty. Going through life with the intention to declutter, but never actually doing it, is an invisible mooring, an unseen rope, keeping her safely anchored to her personal needs yet distant from the needs of others. Could that be true of us? It might be, if we linger always just a few steps behind a personal goal line of one sort or another. Unreached goals can keep us at the center of our world and hold the needs and problems of others at bay.

For those of us like Hayley—frustrated, discouraged, and ashamed by sin and defeat—our problem might be a misunderstanding about salvation in Christ and what it means to live the Christian life. If we don't understand Scripture's teaching, our struggles are bound to take us up, down, and back again from success to failure, freedom to frustration, patience to anger, exaltation to discouragement, and confidence to shame. Sure, we win a battle here and there, but we hold out little hope for winning the war. We wonder where God is in our struggles and why he doesn't seem to be helping. After all, isn't victory the essence of the Christian life?

Well, the answer is both yes and no. It's yes in the sense that once we've been united to Christ, we are no longer enslaved to sin; it no longer owns us and therefore cannot truly define us. But the answer is no in the sense that the presence of sin is going to pester us until we are perfected in glory.

Even so, living in Jesus makes a world of difference—in this life too. Before we become united to Christ by faith, we are *not able not* to sin; once in Christ, we *are able* not to sin. So why do we?

We continue to sin because, although we've been freed from sin's penalty and power, complete freedom from its presence awaits the next life.[4] The apostle Paul, who clearly experienced his own struggles with besetting sin, puts it like this:

> I do not do the good I want, but the evil I do not want is what I keep on doing. Now if I do what I do not want, it is no longer I who do it, but sin that dwells within me. So I find it to be a law that when I want to do right, evil lies close at hand. For I delight in the law of God, in my inner being, but I see in my members another law waging war against the law of

my mind and making me captive to the law of sin that dwells in my members. Wretched man that I am! Who will deliver me from this body of death? (Rom. 7:19–24)

Can you relate to that? I bet you can. Because no matter how long we've walked with the Lord, we can all relate.

So returning to our earlier question—Isn't victory the essence of the Christian life?—the answer depends on what we hope to achieve. Don Matzat writes:

All the frustration that is experienced by those who search for a changed life and victory over sin is based on a wrong diagnosis of the human condition. We erroneously believe that God is in the repair business, that he compassionately repairs human lives like a friendly father fixing his children's broken toys. We make up a list of our specific problems and go about seeking the Lord for specific solutions, but nothing ever gets checked off the list, and it seemingly never ends.[5]

That gets to the heart of our frustration, doesn't it? And one reason for this frustration is that we read and hear so often today that this is exactly what God is—a divine repairman. We need discerning eyes to see where this wrong view of God comes at us and to know what a "changed life" really looks like through the lens of God's Word.

So what about you? If there's sin in your life that you can't seem to overcome or a personal goal you can't quite reach, perhaps it's because, as in Zoe's case, it's rooted in a hidden desire to stay self-centered. Or, like Hayley, maybe you've become so fixated on overcoming a particular sin that you no longer see past the sin to the Savior himself. In either case, when our goals begin and end with ourselves, frustration and discouragement are sure to set in, and we're likely to wind up looking for relief in some other way—a new method or program or book or teaching through which the Lord might empower us. And when we've reached this point, we've made ourselves vulnerable to a lot of unbiblical teaching.

Discern

According to Jesus, we are branches:

> I am the true vine, and my Father is the vinedresser. Every branch in me that does not bear fruit he takes away, and every branch that does bear fruit he prunes, that it may bear more fruit. (John 15:1–2)

Some of us have been led to believe that the fruit Jesus was speaking about here is personal strength or power. But *Christ's* power is the nutrient the branches receive. All the power lies in the vine itself. The centrality of Christ for living the Christian life has gotten buried in recent years by a way of thinking about Christianity called "moralistic therapeutic deism." It's a cumbersome term, but it's important to grasp, because it's everywhere, even within churches.

A Growing Danger

Moralistic therapeutic deism includes the belief that the primary goal of life is personal happiness and a positive self-image. God is viewed as rather distant from our day-to-day lives but available to solve problems and help us feel good about ourselves.[6] But that god is not the God of the Bible, nor does this pattern of teaching even come close to the walk of faith set out for us in Scripture.

We see its influence on a woman who, feeling overwhelmed by cares and responsibilities on a particularly challenging day, looks to herself and her friends for the strength to persevere:

I might feel like I'm not doing anything well, but it doesn't make it true. The fact that I have weaknesses doesn't make everything about me weak. I have plenty of strengths.

All I have to do is ask a couple of my friends or my family members to help me see what I do well. I can celebrate those, and then get a plan for bettering things that need improvement. I can start by identifying one thing to improve on this month. And do a little toward making that one thing better.[7]

Evaluating ourselves by our *self* ultimately gets us nowhere, and the opinion of friends takes us only so far. But trying to harness the Lord's power for our self-improvement projects dishonors the Lord, and it's a recipe for discouragement.

As 2 Corinthians 12:9 teaches, God's power is made perfect in weakness. When I'm sinking in thoughts of inadequacy . . . I remember that my ability is not based on what I can do. My ability and strength come from the One who can do all things. With the Lord working in me and through my weaknesses, I can feel the transformation from being overpowered to empowered taking place.[8]

Can you see the problem there? She co-opts the Lord's power for herself. Yes, the Lord does say that power is made perfect in weakness, but it's *his* power that gets perfected. Notice how wrong thinking about Scripture has crept in: "*My* ability and strength come from the One who can do all things."

The author takes the Bible passage out of context and therefore misses the whole point. Power and strength are always, ever, and only the Lord's. He works his power through us, but he doesn't empower *us*. Do you see the difference? Surely she meant to encourage her readers, but in this article, at least, she misses the mark because she doesn't consider the context of the passage. The actual takeaway from 2 Corinthians 12:1–10 is that God at times leaves us in difficult situations in order to humble our hearts and show us through the difficulty that *he* is strong. So the teaching of the verse she cites is actually the opposite of the encouragement she seeks to draw from it. And in so doing, she entrenches her readers in the very frustration they are so desperately seeking to escape.

Owen Strachan has this to say:

> Too many people today tragically follow a fairy tale god. The God of Scripture is not our life coach. He is our Lord. We're used to this word [Lord] as Christians, and so it loses its edge. This divine title signifies that God is our master. He is our sovereign. He is our ruler. He sets the tone for right and wrong. He calls us to account for our sin.[9]

Wrong teaching on this point is why so many of us believe that Christian discipleship is synonymous with self-improvement. But true Christian discipleship is a call to die, not to improve. It's what Jesus was getting at when he said, "Whoever loves his life loses it, and whoever hates his life in this world will keep it for eternal life" (John 12:25).

Believing that discipleship is centered on us—that it's all about God helping us to be a better *us*—is why we are surprised to discovered that it was Ben Franklin, not Jesus, who said, "God helps those who help themselves." Franklin's unbiblical adage is grounded in the belief that God does his part if we do ours, that God doesn't save individuals until they first choose to be saved, and that the channels of God's blessings remain open so long as we work hard to be decent people. And where this thinking dominates, so does a faith-quenching drive for self-improvement.

Flourish

When it comes to frustration over failure, we have to realize the difference between the question that plagues Hayley and tempts us—"Why won't God help me?"—and the question Paul asks in Romans 7—"Who will deliver me from this body of death?" We ask *why*, whereas Paul asks *who*. Our question exposes our self-focus; Paul's reveals faith. Ours is curved inward; Paul's is focused upward, which is why he finds the answer: "Thanks be to God through Jesus Christ our Lord!" (v. 25). He joyfully declares the answer, and then he goes on to explain his hope:

> There is therefore now no condemnation for those who are in Christ Jesus. For the law of the Spirit of life has set you free in Christ Jesus from the law of sin and death. (Rom. 8:1–2)

In this weighty passage (Rom. 7:19–8:2), Paul is explaining that first and foremost we need to be rescued from God's wrath. And this is what Christ has done through his death on the cross. God's wrath against us has been permanently, eternally removed, and as a result we can count on being rescued from failure. But until Christ's payment for sin has been reckoned to our personal account, the little victories we experience are no different from covering a malignant tumor with a Band-Aid. Until the righteousness of Christ has been applied to us, we remain under "the law of sin and death." When we are united to Christ, we come under a different law altogether—"the law of the Spirit of life"—which progressively frees us from the tyranny of repetitive defeat. So Paul shows us, first, that we are forgiven, and because we've been forgiven, we are now free.

Transformed

So if we are *in* Christ, we can stop focusing first on what we want to change about ourselves and consider instead how God has already changed us. Given that our eternal destiny is set and that the Lord is on our side in every battle, there is no need for chronic frustration, anger, or discouragement when we lose a particular battle. In fact, there's actually much of God's mercy in our ongoing struggle and, yes, even in our failures. God works through struggle and failure to drive us out of ourselves to depend on him so that we can really live. Grasping this truth helps us understand why Jesus calls us "branches":

> I am the true vine, and my Father is the vinedresser. Every branch in me that does not bear fruit he takes away, and every branch that does bear fruit he prunes, that it may bear more fruit. Already you are clean because of the word that I have spoken to you. Abide in me, and I in you. As the branch cannot bear fruit by itself, unless it abides in the vine, neither can you, unless you abide in me. I am the vine; you are the branches. Whoever abides in me and I in him, he it is that bears much fruit, for apart from me you can do nothing. (John 15:1–5)

We are not the vinedresser or the vine. We are simply branches, utterly dependent on the vine for every aspect of life and fruitfulness. We haven't been saved in order to maximize our personal potential and become better versions of ourselves. If that's what we're after, no wonder we're frustrated, angry, and discouraged in the fight. Being united to Christ the vine doesn't improve our *self*—it transforms that self to look and think and act like him.

In fact, that self we want so much to change isn't even there anymore. Christ took that *self* with him when he died, and he did it in such a way that we actually died too:

> Do you not know that all of us who have been baptized into Christ Jesus were baptized into his death? (Rom. 6:3)

That's why self-improvement is fruitless—we can't improve something that has died! Instead, we are called to a whole new focus:

> We were buried therefore with him by baptism into death, in order that, just as Christ was raised from the dead by the glory of the Father, we too might walk in newness of life. (Rom. 6:4)

The way out of the bondage of self-improvement is to recognize that in Christ, there is none of that old self left to improve. We can simply let go of all that. This is what it means to "die to self." It's not about fixing our bad habits; it's letting go of everything about ourselves—the good, the beautiful, the bad, and the ugly—and cooperating with God's Spirit as he begins the lifelong process of making us resemble Christ himself.

How about those bad habits we want to change? Frustration will be replaced with peace and joy when we begin to live out of our changed status. We went with Christ into his death, but then we were raised with him from the dead, which gives us a whole new reality from which to frame our goals.

At the same time, new life in Christ doesn't mean we just sit back passively while God transforms us. Our impulse to "improve" is still good, but by the work of the Spirit, it has been reoriented toward God and centered on Christ. That's what enables us to fight against sin and grow godly character now and for the rest of our lives.

> If then you have been raised with Christ, seek the things that are above, where Christ is, seated at the right hand of God. Set your minds on things that are above, not on things that are on earth. For you have died, and your life is hidden with Christ in God. When Christ who is your life appears, then you also will appear with him in glory. (Col. 3:1–4)

Real Discipleship

So how do we go from the old, fruitless self-improvement goals to new, Christ-centered ones? In the nitty-gritty of daily life, we need to know how these important spiritual truths translate into practical reality. In the passage we just looked at, Colossians 3:1–4, Paul tells us how. First, we seek "things that are above," which means we make God's priorities our priorities. Second, we set our minds on Christ and all that Scripture sets out for us about life in God's kingdom. Paul shows in some of his other letters the link between our minds and spiritual growth:

> Those who live according to the flesh set their minds on the things of the flesh, but those who live according to the Spirit set their minds on the things of the Spirit. For to set the mind on the flesh is death, but to set the mind on the Spirit is life and peace. (Rom. 8:5–6)

And we have this in Romans 12:

> I appeal to you therefore, brothers, by the mercies of God, to present your bodies as a living sacrifice, holy and acceptable to God, which is your spiritual worship. Do not be conformed to this world, but be transformed by the renewal of your mind, that by testing you may discern what is the will of God, what is good and acceptable and perfect. (vv. 1–2)

Improving ourselves is not the sacrifice the Lord calls us to. It's to forget ourselves altogether and live for him instead. We can't do it ourselves, but in Christ we can do it increasingly as we immerse our minds in the things of God—in his Word, by his ways, and with his people. Those who make this their goal are promised no regrets; in fact, they will come to see that switching their focus from themselves to Christ leads to the fullness of life that's been elusive for so long.

Discipleship is not first about doing, but about becoming. Yes, of course we are to do, but in Christ, what we do flows out of what we've already become. In other words, we don't *do* to become. We *become* in order to do. Discipleship is simply the Spirit-enabled process of turning away from sin in all its out-workings and coming more and more to resemble the Savior. You can ditch self-improvement and pursue the fruit of salvation, because "it is God who works in you, both to will and to work for his good pleasure" (Phil. 2:13).

Set Free from Self-Analysis

Sadie is restless, and she's not quite sure what to do about it. Nothing is terribly wrong; it's just that everything seems so blah. After ten years of marriage, she counts herself blessed by the love of her husband. He is unfailingly kind, considerate of her wishes, and patient with her increasing bouts of moodiness. But when Sadie is honest with herself, she has to admit she's a bit bored by his even-keeled temperament. There's nothing there to excite her passions anymore.

The daily routine has also become monotonous, and a tight budget restricts even minimal changes, much less something significant. A weekend getaway would help tremendously, Sadie imagines, but she'd settle for the simple pick-me-up of a new sweater to get her through the remaining winter weeks.

Until recently, Sadie anticipated weekends as a welcome break from the workaday tedium, but weekends involve church, which lately has served only to fuel her restlessness. Same liturgy, same people, same problems—she just doesn't get anything out of it anymore.

"There's got to be more to life," she recently confided to friends over coffee.

"I don't think your life is the problem," one friend replied. "It sounds to me like you're depressed. Maybe your serotonin levels are too low."

"I always thought you played it safe by marrying George," said another friend. "He's a nice guy for sure, but he's never had your passion for life or your drive to experience all it offers. I hate to say it, but this marriage holds you back. It's okay to acknowledge that you made a mistake. Better now than after you have kids."

Her friend from church finally spoke up. "None of that is right! Your walk with God seems ho-hum because you're not trusting him with all this. God loves you! Have you stopped believing he wants your happiness? He will guide you into exciting new paths if you'll believe him for it."

So which is it? Is Sadie's marriage the problem, or a hormonal imbalance, or a failure to trust God for happiness? And which of Sadie's friends is right—or are none of them?

Dig

Who am I? What do I want? What do I feel? Directing our lives by means of those questions leads to chaos. That's because the answers that seem best today are likely to seem all wrong when we assess our feelings tomorrow, and over time we become paralyzed by the impossible task of determining which choices today will make us happiest tomorrow, and the tomorrow after that.

In the course of writing this chapter, I came across an article that summarizes so well what I'm trying to say here:

An obsessive preoccupation with what others will think and a paralyzing fear of failure go hand in hand, and both are symptoms of a hyper-examined life. Many living a hyper-examined life will flit and float from job to job, from friend to friend, from place to place. This may seem adventurous at first, but what's often behind this rootlessness is a compulsive need for satisfaction in every season of life. Instead of losing themselves in the joys of the mundane, the regular, and the everyday, these wandering souls constantly search their own emotional state for happiness—not realizing that such preoccupation with self is exactly what tends to kill happiness in the first place.[10]

The cause of Sadie's restlessness isn't her marriage or her routine or her church. She's restless because she's made her emotions the measure of her well-being. In the process, she is damaging not only her life and relationships but also her faith. Sadie's problem is compounded by well-meaning but misguided friends whose advice merely drives her further into herself and away from the God of Scripture.

It's natural to want to steer our lives along paths that promise happiness. After all, God is the one who created us with the capacity to be happy. But happiness is merely a fruit, a by-product, of something outside of ourselves. We too easily make it the be-all, end-all pursuit of life when, in reality, it comes only as we pursue the Lord himself. So if we fixate on happiness itself, it will elude us all our days.

When feelings rule, we are in danger of thinking that whatever makes us feel good must be God's will, and we then direct the compass of our lives and our prayer requests toward the circumstances that seem most likely to deliver it. When feelings rule, they determine the choices we make (or don't) and the people we serve (or don't). When feelings rule, the truths of God's Word are twisted to suit our desires, and walking in his ways goes only as far as our emotional comfort zone. The result is an unfruitful and chaotic life. Peace and stability come from reorienting ourselves—including our feelings—outward and upward.

Discern

The preeminence of feelings has, in recent years, gone so far as to dictate the laws of our land. In some places it is now illegal for a business owner to conduct operations in any manner that might offend customers' feelings. There are also new laws that safeguard self-determined gender identity. A man is allowed to use the ladies' room because he *feels* that he is a woman, and people must label him as a *her* or risk being ostracized or fired. These laws indicate that the traditional understanding of morality has been flipped upside down in order to guard the feelings of particular subcultures. Mainstream society increasingly believes that it's immoral to stand against gay marriage and a woman's right to choose and to expose college students to polarizing ideas. All this echoes the apostle Paul, who said that such people "not only do [evil things] but give approval to those who practice them" (Rom. 1:32).

The devastation of all this on today's Post-Millennials, the so-called Generation Z, is already visible. An increasing number of colleges and universities offer "safe spaces" and bubble-wrap rooms where students can retreat from upsetting ideas and mold Play-Doh into cartoon characters. It doesn't take an Ivy League education to figure out that this does nothing to prepare young people for the rigors of life in the real world, yet some of today's most academically prestigious institutions are leading these initiatives. The loudest cultural cry today is this demand that the *feelings* of individuals be safeguarded at any cost.

Feelings and Faith

All this has led to a radical shift in our thinking as Christians, thinking about ourselves and about what it means to be a Christian. No small number of self-help resources, including some from evangelical publishers, reflect the cultural mind-set and guide us, however subtly, to seek first not what's best for our community or church or even our family but what we deem best for ourselves. As a result, we don't see anything wrong with aiming more at personal gratification than at God's glory in the plans and choices we make, in some part because we believe that our earthly happiness is the primary way God's glory is showcased. Here's a sample from a popular book:

> Our happy God desires happy children. You are the *imago dei*. You carry the DNA of your happy and holy God. . . . God is the inventor of happiness and the chief spreader of it. When you desire happiness, you are not a pleasure-seeking heretic. You are responding to something built into your soul. Your desire to live happy is not a flaw. It is your soul's memory of the original paradise, etched and alive in you. . . . Thus I pray, "Your happy kingdom come, on earth as it is in heaven." To be sure, our unhappiness and frowns will be confiscated at the gates of heaven. Why don't we get a head start on our happiness inheritance now? Yes, God commands us to pick up our crosses and walk the narrow way home. . . . Some of the best lessons we learn in life will come in the hardest, unhappiest places on earth. . . . But we don't find God only in the hard. We find him also in the happy. *This discovery of our happy Jesus caused me to read Scripture in a whole new way and to examine my own life through the prism of Christ's happiness.* This discovery made me feel alive and warm—a bit glittery on the inside.[11]

We don't find God only in difficulty—that's certainly true. But when happiness is our primary aim, we can be tempted to read Scripture through that lens, twisting its truth in the process. The Bible indicates from beginning to end that happiness in the here and now is *not* God's primary objective for his people. In fact, he cares so much about our eternal happiness that he will sacrifice our earthly happiness if necessary to ensure it. Certainly God takes no delight in our misery—he cares a great deal about how we feel. But his intentions for our happiness are radically different from what we read in some current best sellers. Here's how God makes us happy:

> In him we have obtained an inheritance, having been predestined according to the purpose of him who works all things according to the counsel of his will, *so that we who were the first to hope in Christ might be to the praise of his glory.* (Eph. 1:11–12)

As we see there, God's aim, which he works in and through our lives, is his own glory, and through his work in our lives, he reveals this glory to us and the world around us. In other words, God's glory *is* our happiness, and to the degree that we fixate on him instead of on how we feel, we will come to know firsthand how true this is.

That's why we can stop taking our emotional temperature all the time. Our feelings don't determine our well-being, so there's no need to manipulate our lives to feel good. Christ has freed us from all such inward searching and outward demanding. We simply aren't meant to waste our lives in pursuit of personal pleasure, because God is everything, and all our various dissatisfactions and disappointments are designed to make this clear.

We learn this from all God's dealings with his people in the Bible.

Consider Your Ways

If you are familiar with Old Testament history, then it's likely you know what happened to God's people when they refused to heed his many warnings of judgment and repent of their sin—they were taken away from their homeland and forced to live in Babylon for many years. We call this time in Israel's history "the exile." After seventy years, God's people were permitted to go home, but when they returned, they found their city, the once-glorious Jerusalem, in ruins. Worst of all, the temple had been destroyed. This was a huge deal because in those days the temple was the place where God met with his people. So the returned exiles began the arduous task of rebuilding it, but the work was hard, and they met with one obstacle after another.

Discouragement set in, and over time their rebuilding efforts became half-hearted and then fizzled out altogether as they turned their attention to other prospects that provided more immediate gratification. Before long, they were completely absorbed in the task of rebuilding their own houses rather than the Lord's house and in pursuing a pleasurable lifestyle. But these efforts proved disappointing as well. The people had come home, but they were still unhappy. That's when Haggai the prophet came to them with a word from the Lord:

> Is it a time for you yourselves to dwell in your paneled houses, while this house [the temple] lies in ruins? Now, therefore, thus says the LORD of hosts: Consider your ways. You have sown much, and harvested little. You eat, but you never have enough; you drink, but you never have your fill. You clothe yourselves, but no one is warm. And he who earns wages does so to put them into a bag with holes. (Hag. 1:4–6)

God asks them to think, to give thought to what they are living for. They have put their own houses ahead of his, the enjoyment of personal pleasures above the pleasure of his presence. Here, he is the one calling for some self-analysis. He is opening their eyes to the fact that their pursuit of the good life isn't paying off. Every pleasure they've grabbed has proven disappointing.

Then the call to self-analysis comes to them again:

> Thus says the LORD of hosts: Consider your ways. Go up to the hills and bring wood and build the house, that I may take pleasure in it and that I may be glorified, says the LORD. You looked for much, and behold, it came to little. And when you brought it home, I blew it away. Why? declares the LORD of hosts. Because of my house that lies in ruins, while each of you busies himself with his own house. (Hag. 1:7–9)

That is the sort of self-analysis that leads somewhere, the sort that God calls us to undertake. Biblical self-analysis directs us away from ourselves and toward God. In Haggai's day, an accurate assessment of circumstances was God's instrument to open the eyes of people's hearts to understand why God wasn't blessing their efforts to prosper. In fact, he was blocking those efforts.

Their paneled houses weren't the primary problem. God's concern was that they prioritized those houses and the rest of their creature comforts ahead of him and his glory. If they would put God first, their circumstances would change, and God would be with them as they applied themselves to finish the work he had called them to do (v. 13). That's always how it works—God's claim on our life is meant to be lived out in the strength he supplies.

In Haggai's day, the people weren't to look backward at past blessings, or inward at their moods and desires, but forward, with their eyes on him alone. So the people listened and got to work on the Lord's business, and here's what happened:

> Consider from this day onward, from the twenty-fourth day of the ninth month. Since the day that the foundation of the LORD's temple was laid, consider: Is the seed yet in the barn? Indeed, the vine, the fig tree, the pomegranate, and the olive tree have yielded nothing. *But from this day on I will bless you.* (Hag. 2:18–19)

Jesus said something similar much later on: "Seek first the kingdom of God and his righteousness, and all these things will be added to you" (Matt. 6:33). If we are dissatisfied with how our lives are working out, could this be why? Are we so caught up in shaping our lives to feel happy that we've lost sight of God's claim on our life? Self-analysis is good and right when we do it under the light of Scripture. It's destructive and sinful when the aim of all that internal rooting around is merely personal happiness.

Flourish

If we've been chasing paths of happiness that never deliver what they promise, we're well positioned to heed the call of Haggai: "Consider your ways" (1:7). For some of us, that means asking, "What am I doing?" rather than, "How do I feel?" For others, it means examining the possibility that biblical discipleship has taken a deep slide down our priority list.

Jesus's words about seeking first God's kingdom are found in his Sermon on the Mount, and this particular section of his sermon (Matt. 6:19–34) pinpoints what we've been covering here. "Do not be anxious about your life," he says (v. 25), and isn't that exactly what we are—anxious—when we're entangled in our emotional well-being? Jesus doesn't leave us hanging there, with a command that seems impossible to obey. He tells us that we can stop obsessing about ourselves because God already knows everything we need (v. 32), and he provides for his people (vv. 26, 30). God delights to bless those who trust him (v. 33), and letting go of our self-pursuits and putting him first is most definitely a step of faith. We can't have it both ways, he says. We can serve either the kingdom of God or our craving for personal happiness: "No one can serve two masters, for either he will hate the one and love the other, or he will be devoted to the one and despise the other" (v. 24), and the one we choose reveals what we love most, "for where your treasure is, there your heart will be also" (v. 21).

Analyze This!

Trusting in the Lord frees us from the kind of self-analysis that rises no higher than our emotions and desires, and it guides us to participate in the kind of analysis that leads to fruitful living because it is governed by God's Word and aided by the Holy Spirit. And the Bible provides us with some specifics for this good kind of self-analysis and for where it leads us.

Fruitful self-analysis leads to a right view of reality:

Who *considers* the power of your anger,
and your wrath according to the fear of you?
So teach us to number our days
that we may get a heart of wisdom. (Ps. 90:11–12)

Then I *considered* all that my hands had done and the toil
I had expended in doing it, and behold, all was vanity and a

striving after wind, and there was nothing to be gained under the sun. (Eccles. 2:11)

In the day of prosperity be joyful, and in the day of adversity *consider*: God has made the one as well as the other, so that man may not find out anything that will be after him. (Eccles. 7:14)

If anyone thinks he is something, when he is nothing, he deceives himself. But let each one *test* his own work, and then his reason to boast will be in himself alone and not in his neighbor. (Gal. 6:3–4)

Fruitful self-analysis reveals areas of sin and where repentance is needed, thereby awakening us to our deep need for the Savior:

> Let us test and *examine our ways,*
> and return to the LORD! (Lam. 3:40)

Fruitful self-analysis reveals whether we truly believe the gospel:

> *Examine yourselves,* to see whether you are in the faith. Test yourselves. Or do you not realize this about yourselves, that Jesus Christ is in you?—unless indeed you fail to meet the test! (2 Cor. 13:5)

The godly kind of self-analysis actually directs us away from our earthly lives and increasingly toward Christ and our life in him:

> So you also must *consider* yourselves dead to sin and alive to God in Christ Jesus. (Rom. 6:11)

> Whoever . . . eats the bread or drinks the cup of the Lord in an unworthy manner will be guilty concerning the body and blood of the Lord. Let a person *examine* himself,

then, and so eat of the bread and drink of the cup. (1 Cor. 11:27–28)

Because he himself has suffered when tempted, he is able to help those who are being tempted. Therefore, holy brothers, you who share in a heavenly calling, *consider* Jesus, the apostle and high priest of our confession. (Heb. 2:18–3:1)

Consider him who endured from sinners such hostility against himself, so that you may not grow weary or faint-hearted. (Heb. 12:3)

As the Spirit refocuses the eyes of our heart, turning our inward gaze outward and upward, our desires change and we become passionate about God and his concerns:

Only fear the LORD and serve him faithfully with all your heart. For *consider* what great things he has done for you. (1 Sam. 12:24)

Blessed is the one who *considers* the poor!
　　In the day of trouble the LORD delivers him. (Ps. 41:1)

The wicked lie in wait to destroy me,
　　but I *consider* your testimonies. (Ps. 119:95)

Go to the ant, O sluggard;
　　consider her ways, and be wise. (Prov. 6:6)

Consider the ravens: they neither sow nor reap, they have neither storehouse nor barn, and yet God feeds them. Of how much more value are you than the birds! (Luke 12:24)

Let us *consider* how to stir up one another to love and good works. (Heb. 10:24)

Remember your leaders, those who spoke to you the word of God. *Consider* the outcome of their way of life, and imitate their faith. (Heb. 13:7)

A life curved inward, analyzing and evaluating every mood change and desire, is a stunted, joyless life. Why live there even one more day? Christ is where fullness is found, as he promised: "I came that they may have life and have it abundantly" (John 10:10).

Set Free from Self-Indulgence

Self-care has become a thing. The trend got traction by appealing to necessity—you can't care for others if you don't first care for yourself. So before we can love our husband and children or care for the needs of the hurting or exercise our spiritual gifts, we must tend to our physical, psychological, and emotional selves. Certainly it's wise to be good self-stewards, but the way in which it's trending often runs counter to the stewardship advocated by Jesus: "Whoever seeks to preserve his life will lose it, but whoever loses his life will keep it" (Luke 17:33). In light of Jesus's teaching, some of what goes into today's self-care trend is more along the lines of plain old self-indulgence.

When the topic of self-indulgence is raised, those of us who live in societies marked by luxury think primarily of overeating. But overeating is merely one facet of self-indulgence. Self-indulgence is all that the term implies—it's indulging the self.

Dig

So what's the big deal? Self-indulgence doesn't seem so bad when we hold it up to sins like racism and murder. In fact, opportunities for self-indulgence are viewed as a blessing. It's a reward for hard work, a celebration of personal achievement, and an entrenched belief that "you deserve a break today." Oh, sure, we can take it too far, as the scales or the low bank balance might indicate, but overall, we see self-indulgence as good for us if we keep it in check. This thinking is why we miss the full import of Paul's words about a certain type of woman: "She who is self-indulgent is dead even while she lives" (1 Tim. 5:6).

Paul wrote those words while he was advising Timothy about the care of widows in the church, and he instructs that the self-indulgent among them were to be barred from receiving practical aid. The fact that the church was to withhold aid from these widows sheds light on the seriousness of self-indulgence, but even more sobering is the link Paul makes there between self-indulgence and spiritual death. It's clear here that those who live for themselves and for the gratification of their fleshly, earthbound appetites can't simultaneously live for Christ. Even if we don't practice a full-scale overindulgent lifestyle, we are likely to get a taste of the sort of death Paul had in mind here when we do overindulge. When we sate ourselves on the things of this world—pleasures and comforts of whatever kind—we become spiritually sluggish. Our prayer life, our Scripture reading, and all the delights of belonging to God seem distant and dull when we prioritize our time and activities around gratifying our appetites. Have we not all had at least a taste of Paul's words? "She who is self-indulgent is dead even while she lives."

Discern

We understand what it means to overindulge our bodily appetites. It's harder to recognize the overindulgence of our minds and emotions and the means by which we do so. As we look at how the self-care trend has grown into a booming industry, we get an idea.

Strategies for Stress

We can see the trend in the recent coloring-book craze, the popularity of which, in some measure, is the result of how it has been tied to self-care. There is an endless selection of adult coloring books, and there are even coloring Bibles for those whose devotional life could use an exhilarating boost. Over the past few years, publishers have been cranking them out to where sales of those coloring books have ranked them high on best-seller lists, in some cases because they are marketed as a means of spiritual growth. Tim Challies writes:

> Somehow, coloring has progressed from a hobby to a form of spirituality, from a pastime to a spiritual discipline. . . . God is delighted when we find delight in hobbies. But there's no heavenly or earthly reason to elevate coloring to the realm of prayer, meditation, or spiritual discipline. The same is true of any other hobby or any other activity. When coloring becomes a form of spirituality, it becomes both distracting and dangerous.[12]

There is certainly nothing wrong or overindulgent about sitting down to relax with some crayons, but there is if we come to *depend* on coloring books to reduce our stress. And if we lose interest in Bible reading without colored pencils, coloring has become way more than it ever should be. What begins as self-care can morph into habits of laziness, where we are unwilling to exert ourselves without some pleasurable comfort as an accompaniment.

At the other end of the spectrum are the overexerted—exhausted moms and others whose work goes around the clock. Their patience is tried and tested on a daily basis, so grabbing a few minutes of peace and quiet by any available means is surely a blessing, one to take advantage of whenever possible. Self-indulgence becomes a factor, however, when we allow those unreasonably busy seasons to make us selfish and demanding in our fight for "me time." And while there are certainly situations and relationships in which we need to set limits and safeguard our sanity, we won't flourish if we miss how God is at work in our hectic routine:

> Count it all joy, my brothers, when you meet trials of various kinds, for you know that the testing of your faith produces steadfastness. And let steadfastness have its full effect, that you may be perfect and complete, lacking in nothing. (James 1:2–4)

James sees hardships, which include chaotic life seasons, as tests of faith in which God is at work to mature and enrich us. If we miss that truth, if instead we panic about our schedule as we listen to and absorb all the warnings of failing to practice self-care, we can lose sight of James's words or even attempt to refuse a test of faith by seeking a remedy that offers a more immediate payoff.

When it comes to managing exhaustion, some women have resorted to the backyard "she shed," a private, self-made outbuilding—the female version of the traditional man cave—in which to escape the daily chaos. Surely much good can come from retreating to a private space for some quiet hours, and a quick search of Pinterest shows just how creative and beautiful such spaces can be. So desiring a she shed isn't self-indulgent (although it might be, if you consider the tens of thousands of dollars spent on some of them), but it *is* self-indulgent to demand one. And we fail to care for ourselves or anyone else if we come to believe that a backyard hideaway is a prerequisite for cooking dinner with kindness.

Some pursue self-care not through solitary hours but by seeking advice. And this is good! God designed us to need one another, to both give and receive guidance and help for life's many challenges. But it's not so good if we mostly seek it in self-help books and spiritually based websites rather than in a local church. Belonging to a particular body of believers—not only gathering for Sunday worship but also doing life together—is God's primary provision for our growth and encouragement. God designed the church to function like a body, where each part works to support all the other parts, producing overall good health (see 1 Cor. 12:12–27; Eph. 4:11–16). So of course we can search for and find some good counsel apart from our church, but we want to guard against allowing that outside counsel to replace our church. For exhausted moms and CEOs and every woman, God intends our flourishing to occur primarily in a local church context.

Do We Need a Life Coach?

The downside of evangelical websites—even the sound ones—is that such easy access to helpful content has hidden from our view the vitality that comes only through real, nonvirtual church life. But websites aren't the only distraction. We can find ourselves pulled away from the give-and-take of church life by a full-scale embrace of a profession called "life coaching." We are encouraged today to get established with our own life coach, someone trained and certified to guide us to become all we can be.

Those who become life coaches desire to help and encourage others to maximize their present and future potential, and specifically Christian life coaches attempt to undertake this by rooting their coaching in biblical principles. But the concept overall can interfere with how the church is meant to function. We are called as a collective body to aid one another, not in maximizing personal potential but in becoming more Christ-centered and kingdom-focused.

Certainly there is a place for life coaching, and no doubt it helps many. One Christian college has offered a certification program called Life Coach Training Basics, which is designed to teach students to aid "justice-involved adults" seeking to reenter society following incarceration.[13] That's a terrific mission, and very different from the kind of life coaching that's practiced by some self-care advocates. If we are considering engaging in life coaching, either to train or be trained, it's wise to examine whether the program we have in view will drive us out of ourselves or farther inward.

The primary pitfall to avoid is the view of Jesus as life coach as shown here:

> When Jesus, your personal Coach, looks at you, he will ask you one question: "What do you want me to do for you?" That was the question he asked again and again in his ministry. . . . Jesus is asking you to focus now. All the power is here. All the goodwill is here. All the intent is here right now. It is up to you to decide on who you want to be and what you want to be about in this world.[14]

Jesus is not a life coach. He is Savior and Lord. And it is not up to us to decide who we want to be in this world. We've been called as disciples and servants.

Indulgence or Necessity?

The trendy self-care movement can slide us so easily off the path of true biblical discipleship. Scripture calls us to lay down our lives and follow Jesus, but we hear increasingly that Jesus laid down his life to maximize our potential and make our lives more comfortable. Marshall Segal writes, "Self-care strategies attempt to apply structure and discipline to 'me-time,' re-centering our world around ourselves . . . , and looking for hope, healing, and stability from some hidden place deep within ourselves."[15]

We see this recentering in how one author describes his book:

> Life is not user-friendly, we all need some instructions along the way. . . . This is a book about the self, first of all, and then how that self, endowed by God with a divine image, can experience self-worth, emotional health, and a strong and vital faith in the face of life's inevitable and irrational pain and suffering. . . . It is the realization of God's gift of personal empowerment and spiritual healing.[16]

What we see there is, in essence, an indulging of the self, and it diminishes God and subtly deifies human beings. But the danger is hard to see when it's packaged as a tool to grow "a strong and vital faith." And those who come to such a book with a limited understanding of Scripture are likely to miss its subtle warping of biblical truth. We have not been "endowed by God with a divine image"; we have been *made* in his image. It might seem that I am quibbling about semantics, but the difference in meaning here is vitally significant, and it's no overstatement to claim that absorbing the wrong message can be a matter of life and death.

Self-indulgence—indulging the self, whether mentally, physically, or emotionally—is increasingly seen as a necessary aspect of coping with life. And more often than not, we live out this belief in how we use God's provisions for day-to-day life. We soothe our loneliness with a chocolate bar and escape anxious care with a bottle of wine. We escape the winter's seasonal affective disorder with a jaunt to the Caribbean. Boredom with the weekly routine can be temporarily assuaged by a day at the spa.

Chocolate and wine and fun weekends are delightful gifts indeed, and God is glorified when we partake with joy and gratitude. But viewing these blessings as necessities is self-indulgent. If we demand them as rights, they will enslave us, evaporating the delight and glory they were meant to convey. No one actually *needs* a spa day or wine or chocolate or even a vacation.

For most of us, vacations—at least, the kind we fantasize about—are a luxury, not a need. Do we believe that? I'm not so sure we do. "I need a vacation"—we all hear it; most of us say it. In the weekly rhythm of life established by God, the proportion allotted for work is significantly higher than that allotted for rest. And the rest allotment doesn't necessitate a cottage at the beach or a backpacking trek through Europe. We see in Scripture times and seasons set aside for refreshment and rejuvenation, but what actually refreshed God's people wasn't beach time but festivals and feasts held in celebration of God's goodness. No doubt God's people in Bible times did enjoy a scaled-down version of our modern vacation, but the point I am trying to make is that the source of rest and refreshment depicted in Scripture is focusing on God and celebrating him in the company of his people. We can and should delight in all kinds of opportunities for exotic vacations and personal refreshment, but insisting upon them as a life-sustaining necessity is oftentimes just plain old self-indulgence.

Self-Indulgence Pitfalls

Overindulgence of our physical appetites is so prevalent today because the means for overindulging are so near at hand. And then, ironically, some of the ways we try to undo the consequences of overindulgence lead us straight into a different type of self-indulgence. So, for example, when we feel the negative effects of eating too much, we can turn around and indulge ourselves in the opposite extreme.

Given the health risks, processed foods have become taboo for many, but short of a genuine health concern, a scrupulous adherence to trendy food rules can in some circumstances be self-indulgent. Avoiding Velveeta and Cool Whip is surely a choice for good health, but is consuming only superfoods like kale and quinoa really so crucial to our well-being? We spend inordinate amounts of time researching and entering into fad diets. We devote ourselves to Whole30 or the ketogenic diet or *The Daniel Plan*, a diet program derived in part from the book of Daniel in the Old Testament.

When God's people were taken captive to Babylon in the sixth century BC, the Babylonian king Nebuchadnezzar came up with a strategy to assimilate a young man named Daniel and other Israelite captives into his culture:

> The king assigned them a daily portion of the food that the king ate, and of the wine that he drank. They were to be educated for three years, and at the end of that time they were to stand before the king. (Dan. 1:5)

But Daniel and his friends resisted the king's rich fare, and they asked the king for a different diet:

> "Test your servants for ten days; let us be given vegetables to eat and water to drink. Then let our appearance and the

appearance of the youths who eat the king's food be observed by you, and deal with your servants according to what you see." So he listened to them in this matter, and tested them for ten days. At the end of ten days it was seen that they were better in appearance and fatter in flesh than all the youths who ate the king's food. So the steward took away their food and the wine they were to drink, and gave them vegetables. (Dan. 1:12–16)

While the name of the diet, *The Daniel Plan*, is based on the character of Daniel rather than on what he ate, some proponents of *The Daniel Plan* use this episode in Daniel 1 as the framework for participating in the diet:

[Daniel] understood God wanted him to live a healthy lifestyle so he could serve God no matter where he was located. Healthy living requires faith as the foundation, trusting that God's way is the best way, while following his prescription for your health.[17]

But if we do a bit more digging about Daniel and his situation, we see that Daniel's request for a limited diet was his way of resisting the temptations of Babylon and of maintaining his identity as a Jew during his time in a foreign land. A healthy diet and lifestyle was not his objective. Here we see again why it is vital to understand a bit about the Bible in its original context before we draw out applications for today. Equipping ourselves with some background about Daniel and his circumstances would help us avoid misunderstanding Daniel's diet as a health issue. In fact, people in Daniel's day didn't even think in those terms.[18]

When we try to plug the Bible's historical events directly into our lives today, we run the danger of misinterpreting what God intends to say to us through those ancient stories. Daniel's story in Scripture teaches us about remaining faithful to the Lord when we are pressured to conform to something ungodly; it does not teach us about serving him better through good health. The principle of good bodily stewardship is certainly true, but we simply don't get that from Daniel.

Proponents of *The Daniel Plan* mean well, and no doubt they desire to honor God. But we see again that taking Scripture out of context in this way can wrongly shape our understanding of the Lord and his purposes for his people, and it risks trivializing the Bible and reducing it to a handbook for better living.

As we seek to deal with the consequences of physical overindulgence—in the case of food, by dieting—we need to guard against the pitfall of more self-indulgence, and this is why our heart plays a vital role. We worry a lot about fat-clogged arteries, but even more important is the spiritual heart, which is ultimately responsible for the overindulgence consequences we're suffering today. Diets are valuable tools for dealing with those consequences, but if our hearts remain unchanged, we are likely to endlessly repeat the binge-diet-binge-diet cycle. If our hearts remain unchanged, any diet we undertake becomes little more than a technique for idol management. The idol I have in mind here isn't food or any other physical pleasure—it's *comfort*.

The Comfort Idol

Self-indulging is how we worship the idol of comfort, and orienting our lives on whatever promises to provide it in the fastest, easiest, most enjoyable way is how we bow down. As with any kind of idol, the appeal to immediate gratification is why self-indulgence snares us.

Over time, an indulgence here and another there, we can no longer see how to cope without our comfort-providing substances. If we've managed social anxiety with alcohol, the prospect of a dry party holds no appeal. If we've suppressed painful emotions with food, hunger pangs can evoke a sense of dread. If we've broken up the tedium of routine with exotic travel, we're likely to go into debt as necessary to ensure the continuation of these regular getaways. Our comforts become a prison of our own making.

Flourish

We often don't see the bars of our self-made prison until we try to change. At some point we become aware that overindulgence has made us sluggish, either physically or spiritually (usually both, because they typically occur together). So with fresh determination, we set out to practice self-control and root out bad habits, and that's when we realize we're stuck. We've been indulging for so long that we simply don't know how to do life without our comforts and coping devices.

How Grace Works

The good news for those in Christ is that we aren't really imprisoned. Jesus broke the power of enslaving habits on the cross, and all the sin of our self-indulgence was paid for there. We have been set free, "for the grace of God has appeared, bringing salvation for all people, training us to renounce ungodliness and worldly passions, and to live self-controlled, upright, and godly lives in the present age" (Titus 2:11–12).

Even so, we are likely to feel imprisoned when we initially try to change and to be tempted to doubt the working of God's grace. But his grace is evidenced in the fact that we even want to change. Were it not for grace, we'd live out our lives devoted to pleasure, crying, "Let us eat and drink, for tomorrow we die!" (see Isa. 22:12–14; 1 Cor. 15:32). Paul explains that grace *trains* us to change ungodly habits; in other words, we have some work to do. Grace trains us to renounce ungodly habits and to be self-controlled. Any kind of training typically involves a process, often an arduous one, and we are unlikely to go the distance unless we are willing for some discomfort. It's the only way to crush the comfort idol. We need to keep in mind that our particular indulgence isn't the idol; comfort is. Indulging is merely the way we worship the comfort god.

So are we willing for a bit of discomfort if it means we can shake off our spiritual sluggishness and grow up in Christ? A comfort-loving scribe once declared to Jesus, "'Teacher, I will follow you wherever you go.' And Jesus said to him, 'Foxes have holes and birds of the air have nests, but the Son of Man has nowhere to lay his head'" (Matt. 8:19–20).

Even though we have to work at change, we aren't left to ourselves in the process: "Walk by the Spirit," Paul instructs, "and you will not gratify the desires of the flesh" (Gal. 5:16). It's really that simple—not easy, but simple. The battle for godliness is fought at precisely this point, because those desires of the flesh ache to be gratified. Paul describes it this way:

> The desires of the flesh are against the Spirit, and the desires of the Spirit are against the flesh, for these are opposed to each other, to keep you from doing the things you want to do. (Gal. 5:17)

When we choose to indulge ourselves rather than to walk by the Spirit, the inevitable result is a big heap of ugly, as Galatians 5:19–21 shows us. Unrestrained sexual desires lead to sexually perverted inclinations. Misuse of food and drink and other substances leads to addiction; justification of sinful emotions such as anger and jealousy destroys relationships. Whenever we indulge in something bad or overindulge in something good, we are not walking by the Spirit, because his leading is always in the opposite direction.

Walk by the Spirit

If we walk by the Spirit, if we are willing to forgo what we've come to rely on for comfort—and willing, for a time, to experience the discomfort that happens in the letting-go process—our cravings to indulge will diminish. The Spirit leads us out of ourselves so that we are no longer preoccupied with how we feel, what we want, and what we think we need, and as we grow, we begin to see that self-preoccupation is what imprisoned us all along.

As we walk by the Spirit, we are led away from ourselves and directed toward Christ. We become increasingly preoccupied with him. In the process, we come to look more like him. We reflect not the consequences of self-indulgence but the fruit of self-control, along with love, joy, peace, patience, kindness, goodness, faithfulness, and gentleness (Gal. 5:22–23). Paul concludes this section of Galatians with a command: "If we live by the Spirit"—and we do, if we've put our faith in Christ— "let us keep in step with the Spirit" (v. 25). The Spirit transforms us, but we are not passive in the process. The zeal we once devoted to indulging ourselves we must now redirect along the path of discipleship.

In his letter to believers in Ephesus, Paul makes a similar contrast between indulging our flesh and walking by the Spirit: "Do not get drunk with wine, for that is debauchery, but be filled with the Spirit" (Eph. 5:18). The point he's making is about more than just drinking. In Paul's day, worshipers of pagan gods thought they could enhance their spiritual experience by consuming alcohol, so Paul wants believers to be absolutely clear that Christianity doesn't work that way. We can't stuff ourselves with earthly things and simultaneously exhibit the fruit of the Spirit.

Here in Ephesians Paul goes on to reveal another facet of the Spirit's fruit—gratitude:

> Do not get drunk with wine, for that is debauchery, but be filled with the Spirit, addressing one another in psalms and hymns and spiritual songs, singing and making melody to the Lord with your heart, *giving thanks always and for everything to God the Father in the name of our Lord Jesus Christ.* (Eph. 5:18–20)

All forms of sinful self-indulgence spring from an ungrateful heart. If we live to gratify ourselves with comfort or pleasure of whatever kind, it's because we believe that God is not enough for us. In some hidden recess of our heart, we judge him insufficient when he fails to meet our personal expectations of what we want and think we deserve. When we are dominated by this belief, we can't possibly recognize that everything we have—friendship, food, shelter, work, health, marriage, singleness, fellowship, talent, and eternal salvation most of all—is a gift.

As we keep in step with the Spirit, our thinking changes, and the craving to self-indulge begins to die. And our hearts are humbled, which enables us to see God for who he is and everything we have as a gift. Gratitude to God—not just words of thanks but a heart-deep belief—makes self-indulgence meaningless. So we aren't in prison after all, if we belong to Christ by faith. We've been set free—gloriously free—from bondage to sin, Satan, and self.

5

Set Free from Self-Condemnation

That thing we said, that thing we did—if only we could take it back. A memory of sharp words spoken in anger, the night we went along with the crowd, or maybe left the crowd and wish we hadn't—the haunting of regret can be relentless. We'd love to erase certain things with a simple stroke of a life "undo" key, but we know all too well that words cannot be unsaid and past events cannot be undone. How can we live well today when we can't shake the past—even the confessed and forgiven past? We trust that we've been forgiven because Christ paid for all our sins when he died on the cross, but the memory isn't erased, and the effects on us and on those we hurt can linger long.

I think, for example, of a long-ago colleague named Amber, who in her teens had given birth to a son she named Jimmy. No father was in the picture, and she'd had to quit school to provide for him. She loved her boy, but she resented him too, first for interrupting and then permanently altering her young life. She was harsh with him at times, even after she regained a bit of freedom when he reached school age. I met Amber about twenty years after Jimmy was born. The day we'd met, I'd inquired about the framed photo of the smiling adolescent on her desk. "Is that your son?"

"Yes," she replied. "It's an old picture."

"Oh? How old is he now? Is he still in school?"

"No. He got into drugs."

"I'm so sorry. I hope he finds the way out of that."

"He won't. He got shot during a drug deal, and he's dead."

It's been years since that conversation, but I'll never forget it. My heart broke for my colleague, but not fully on that particular day. That came some months later during a coffee break with Amber in the lunchroom, when we overheard another colleague express loud dismay about parents who say awful things to their kids. A raised voice filtered above the lunchroom chatter: "Do they not realize they're shaping their children's lives by screaming and telling them they're worthless and stupid?"

Amber was quiet for a moment, and then she looked down and said, "That's what I did to my son."

She opened up during the remainder of our coffee break, which is how I learned the details of Jimmy's birth and short life, and I could see how that day's lunchroom rant on bad parenting had served as a weapon to beat her already-bruised heart. Although she knew God had forgiven her, she just couldn't forgive herself.

Dig

What can help women like Amber and any of us who live under a weight of self-condemnation?

Some carry that weight not because of what they've said or done but because of what others have said and done to them. It's revealed in the woman who regularly puts herself down:

"I'm such a failure!"

"I'm a terrible friend."

"I could never get involved in church. I have nothing to offer."

They've come to believe what they've been told about themselves, perhaps from a very young age.

I think it's safe to assume that the majority of women in the sex trade, whether pornography or prostitution, live under an unbearable weight of self-condemnation. But for most of them, that weight began to press long before their bartering sex for money. No little girl says, "I want to be a prostitute when I grow up." But if she's sexually abused, she might come to believe that's all she's good for. Or if she's abandoned by her father, the message she gets is that no man could ever really love her. Condemnation turned inward so often becomes a self-fulfilling prophecy.

We might also feel condemned when we can't conquer a besetting sin, or when we fail to measure up to the standards we have set for ourselves. To that end, sometimes we fail to distinguish between real, biblically named sin and that which is self-defined. In other words, we view our personal failures as sin, even when God's Word doesn't.

Whether our struggle concerns real sin or the personal failures we define as sin, self-condemnation inhibits us from finding comfort in the gospel. Instead we berate ourselves and become critical and judgmental, not only toward ourselves but toward others too. Such misery is caused not primarily by anything we are doing or failing to do but by our inward curve.

Past sins can dominate our thoughts as we rehearse over and over what we did or said and the hurt we caused. Allowing such thoughts to dominate inhibits us from comprehending how thoroughly the gospel deals with sin and guilt. If we'd only look away from that—away from ourselves altogether—and direct our gaze to Christ in his Word, we'd see that Christ's sacrifice trumps our sin in every respect. Jesus didn't die on the cross for any sin of his. He took on himself our sin—yours and mine—and bore the guilt of it so we don't have to. "There is therefore now no condemnation for those who are in Christ Jesus" (Rom. 8:1). Quite frankly, if God has forgiven us, who are we to condemn ourselves? Christ died for all the sin—past, present, and future—of those who are united to him by faith.

In light of that reality, if we have put our faith in his sufficiency for us, why do we still feel condemned? Maybe we are measuring ourselves by a different standard, one not rooted in God's Word. Scripture is where we learn that failing to reach personal goals isn't necessarily sinful, but having a perfectionist spirit that demands it is. "Come to me," Jesus said, "all who labor and are heavy laden, and I will give you rest. Take my yoke upon you, and learn from me, for I am gentle and lowly in heart, and you will find rest for your souls. For my yoke is easy, and my burden is light" (Matt. 11:28–30).

Discern

Our sins and failures loom too large in our eyes when Christ seems too small, and he is sure to seem small if our view of ourselves obscures our view of him. So that's the first thing we've got to consider if we're weighed down by a sense of condemnation—*Where are we looking?*

Let's analyze those sins and failures that hold our conscience hostage. First, are they actually sins, and who determines what *is* sin? As we've noted, the Lord alone has the authority to declare what is sinful, and he has done so clearly in his Word. Therefore, Scripture is the only standard that matters. So, for example, being overweight isn't a sin, even though the process by which we got there might be. Likewise, skipping the gym isn't a sin, although the reason for skipping might be. In fact, sin is more likely to underlie rigidity to a workout routine than an inclination to skip it. Declining a request to help in the church nursery isn't sinful, but the reason for saying no might be. Switching to a different church isn't a sin, but the reason for switching might be. Whatever the issue, we don't have the authority to declare something as sinful that Scripture does not. So sipping an alcoholic drink isn't a sin. Viewing an R-rated movie isn't a sin. Listening to pop music isn't a sin. From a biblical standpoint, these things are neutral.

Even so, something neutral in general isn't neutral for everyone all the time or to the same degree. The heart can manufacture sin out of anything. The activities of the eyes, the hands, the feet, the imagination, and every other body part are merely the outworking of what's in the heart:

> What comes out of the mouth proceeds from the heart, and this defiles a person. For out of the heart come evil thoughts, murder, adultery, sexual immorality, theft, false witness, slander. These are what defile a person. But to eat with unwashed hands does not defile anyone. (Matt. 15:18–20)

At times the Holy Spirit might put his finger on something that needs to be cut from our lives, a habit or activity that, over the course of time, has become sinful or brought forth other sin. If we ignore these Spirit-directed nudges, knowing them to be reinforced by Scripture, we are going to feel weighed down, just as David did:

> Blessed is the one whose transgression is forgiven,
>> whose sin is covered.
> Blessed is the man against whom the Lord counts no
>> iniquity,
>> and in whose spirit there is no deceit.
> For when I kept silent, my bones wasted away
>> through my groaning all day long.
> For day and night your hand was heavy upon me;
>> my strength was dried up as by the heat of summer.
>> (Ps. 32:1–4)

And as James writes, "Whoever knows the right thing to do and fails to do it, for him it is sin" (James 4:17). Here is where the battle is waged. If we're unwilling to give up some sin or something good that works to provoke us to sin, we will try to coast along unchanged or spin it to look like anything except real sin. And because God is faithful, he presses in with that heavy hand that David writes about. But Spirit-given conviction is very different from the self-condemnation we're addressing here.

Guilty Feelings—or True Guilt?

The self-condemnation I have in mind is the unshakable sense of guilt that can bury us even when we've confessed our sin and turned our back on it. The root of the problem here, as with every topic we're examining in this book, is our focus. We are focusing too much on ourselves—our sins, our failures—rather than on the Lord and his provision for those sins. We forget (or maybe haven't known) that only God has the authority to condemn and the authority to forgive. We have the authority for neither. And the truth is, we *do* deserve condemnation. We *are* guilty. That's why minimizing our sin, telling ourselves it's not that bad, doesn't alleviate those guilty feelings.

Our sin is as bad—in fact, worse—than we know or ever admit to ourselves. I recently heard it said that if we were to see the reality of our sin, we would actually go insane. That's why putting a positive spin on sin in order to feel better doesn't get us anywhere. Our guilty feelings aren't the problem—it's that we *are* guilty. Fleeing to Christ and taking refuge in him is our only hope, and those who do are the only ones who experience freedom from guilt—both its reality and how it makes us feel. For that reason, listening to the message that we simply need to forgive ourselves is spiritually destructive.

The author of one such article recounts that she felt guilty for years following a childhood mishap, even though she'd expressed great remorse for the incident and begged forgiveness the very day it happened. After encountering the offended party years later, who made no mention of that long-ago infraction, the author was finally able to let go, and she writes:

> I had forgiven myself, and I felt free. You see, Jesus has already forgiven us for every wrong thing we have ever done. It's when we aren't willing to forgive ourselves that we put on the chains of guilt and shame.[19]

Certainly she is right in that Jesus has atoned for all the sins of those who put their trust in him, but she makes herself too big in her own eyes by mistakenly requiring self-forgiveness in order to experience freedom from guilt and shame. We do not have the authority to do that. Only God does, which means that our view of ourselves can be rightly defined only by his view of us. If he declares us guilty, we are condemned. If he declares us forgiven, we are free. How we feel about ourselves concerning a past sin—or even a present sin struggle—has no bearing on the actual reality. The author concludes the article on the right note by directing her readers to Jesus:

There is freedom in Christ from the shame we hold onto. There is Hope. Today, come to Jesus and give Him your guilt; give Him your sins. Let Him unlock the shackles that hold you back. I promise, He will take them from you, and you will be free.[20]

That good truth about help and hope in Christ can be easily lost, however, when it appears under the heading of self-forgiveness. The overall concept of self-forgiveness, even when Christ is held out as the answer, is more about freedom from guilty feelings than freedom from actual guilt.

What we focus on defines us, so if our focus is inward, on ourselves, we wind up defining for ourselves whether we are righteous or guilty. When we begin and end with us—with our *self*—we miss the heart of the gospel and never truly find the freedom for which we ache.

The Only Judge That Matters

The most vicious promoter of our self-condemning tendencies and inaccurate thinking about forgiveness is Satan himself. His very name points to this reality—Satan means "accuser" or "adversary." Nowhere is his technique presented more clearly in Scripture than in the vision given to the prophet Zechariah concerning Joshua the high priest. The vision depicts a courtroom scene where Joshua is the defendant. He stands on trial before the angel of the Lord, who is the judge, and the prosecutor is none other than Satan. But Joshua has the best possible defense attorney—the Lord himself. Zechariah writes:

> He showed me Joshua the high priest standing before the angel of the Lord, and Satan standing at his right hand to accuse him. And the Lord said to Satan, "The Lord rebuke you,

O Satan! The LORD who has chosen Jerusalem rebuke you! Is not this a brand plucked from the fire?" (Zech. 3:1–2)

Joshua needs a good attorney because he has come to court dressed in vile, dirty clothes. The filth covering him in the vision was actually excrement, and showing up to court in this attire was no mere breach of etiquette; the clothing defiled Joshua's whole person, making him ritually unclean and unable to carry out his responsibilities as high priest. Joshua's condition meant that God's people had no one to intercede for them on the Day of Atonement. Right there in the courtroom Satan has all the evidence he needs to win his case, which he surely would have done had the Lord not intervened:

> Now Joshua was standing before the angel, clothed with filthy garments. And the angel said to those who were standing before him, "Remove the filthy garments from him." And to him he said, "Behold, I have taken your iniquity away from you, and I will clothe you with pure vestments." And I said, "Let them put a clean turban on his head." So they put a clean turban on his head and clothed him with garments. And the angel of the LORD was standing by. (Zech. 3:3–5)

The Lord intervened first by silencing Satan and then by providing Joshua with clean clothes. Finally, acting as judge, he declared Joshua not guilty. As is true of our legal system today, the not-guilty verdict didn't mean Joshua, the defendant, was innocent. He actually was guilty, and on top of that, his defilement impacted so many of God's people. So Zechariah's vision points forward in time to Christ, the only undefiled high priest in the history of high priests. Joshua was declared not guilty because Christ took that verdict upon himself.

Sin makes us feel like Joshua did when he was covered in filthy clothes. We are clothed—covered—in sin, and it is filthy. And we aren't capable of changing our spiritual wardrobe. Satan loves to point out our filth as he seeks to prosecute us, making accusations and pointing out our defilement before the Judge. But with Christ as our advocate, Satan can't win his case. If we have been united to Christ by faith, we've already been given new clothes, and the filth of our guilt has been stripped away. It doesn't matter what we've done, or how bad it is. In Christ we have a whole new outfit:

> I will greatly rejoice in the LORD;
>> my soul shall exult in my God,
> for he has clothed me with the garments of salvation;
>> he has covered me with the robe of righteousness,
> as a bridegroom decks himself like a priest with a beautiful
>> headdress,
>> and as a bride adorns herself with her jewels. (Isa. 61:10)

The Lord is our judge, but he is also our defender, and he declares us not guilty by reason of his sacrifice for our sin. So we can disregard Satan's accusations. When he brings to mind our sins, when he points out our self-centeredness, our worldliness, and our failures to love, we can tune him out with God's Word:

> Since we have a great priest over the house of God, let us draw near with a true heart in full assurance of faith, with our hearts sprinkled clean from an evil conscience and our bodies washed with pure water. Let us hold fast the confession of our hope without wavering, for he who promised is faithful. (Heb. 10:21–23)

If you think about it, the message we hear today about the need to forgive ourselves plays right into the hands of the evil prosecutor. If he can keep us fixated on ourselves, looking inward for a declaration of not guilty, we won't be able to see our defender and advocate, Christ Jesus.

Flourish

It's clear that we have guilty feelings because we *are* guilty. Even so, our guilty feelings are unreliable. We flourish when we lean on Christ and, as we do, grow in our ability to distinguish true guilt from false. The accuser, Satan, is also a liar, and he will twist truth like a pretzel to trouble our conscience where it's free and to free it where it should be troubled. But our helper, the Holy Spirit, works in our hearts to sort this out as we immerse ourselves in God's Word.

Some of us struggle with self-condemnation because we have a weak conscience. Here's how John MacArthur defines a weak conscience:

> The weakened conscience usually is hypersensitive and over-active about issues that are not sins. Ironically, a weak conscience is more likely to accuse than a strong conscience. Scripture calls this a weak conscience because it is too easily wounded. People with weak consciences tend to fret about things that should provoke no guilt in a mature Christian who knows God's truth.[21]

As we grow in Christ, our conscience matures. As it is divinely reshaped, we have a greater and more enduring experience of freedom as we live out our faith.

Help from Hebrews

We find much in the book of Hebrews to help us train our conscience.[22] One thing we learn there is that before Christ came, no one could have a truly clean conscience, even when high priests such as Joshua offered animals as a sacrifice for sin:

> According to this arrangement [the Old Testament sacrificial system], gifts and sacrifices are offered that cannot perfect the conscience of the worshiper, but deal only with food and drink and various washings, regulations for the body imposed until the time of reformation. (Heb. 9:9–10)

When the high priest took the blood of animals into the Most Holy Place, God accepted it as atonement for people's sin, but it had to be done year after year, because the people continued to sin. Only one sacrifice for sin has ever been good enough so that a single offering was sufficient to clear the guilty once and for all:

> When Christ appeared as a high priest of the good things that have come, . . . he entered once for all into the holy places, not by means of the blood of goats and calves but by means of his own blood, thus securing an eternal redemption. For if the blood of goats and bulls, and the sprinkling of defiled persons with the ashes of a heifer, sanctify for the purification of the flesh, how much more will the blood of Christ, who through the eternal Spirit offered himself without blemish to God, purify our conscience from dead works to serve the living God. (Heb. 9:11–14)

Christ alone can free our conscience, and as we see there in Hebrews, he does it so that we can serve God. In other words, a clean conscience leads to good works. But it doesn't work in reverse— good works do not lead to a clean conscience. Nothing we do can remove real guilt, which is why self-forgiveness is pointless.

When we are united to Christ by faith, the guilt of our sin is over and done with, and the blessings of belonging to him aren't just for later, in the afterlife, but for here and now too. That's what the author of Hebrews wants us to get:

> Therefore, brothers, since we have confidence to enter the holy places by the blood of Jesus, by the new and living way that he opened for us through the curtain, that is, through his flesh, and since we have a great priest over the house of God, let us draw near with a true heart in full assurance of faith, with our hearts sprinkled clean from an evil conscience and our bodies washed with pure water. Let us hold fast the confession of our hope without wavering, for he who promised is faithful. (Heb. 10:19–23)

There's our freedom. *Christ* is faithful—even when we are not. So when those feelings of condemnation suck us down, we get back up and set the gospel in front of our face.

Defined by Christ

The lost aren't the only ones who need the gospel—the saved need this good news too. We need it because we forget, and because Satan is a master prosecutor. We will never outgrow our need for this basic message. In it we find confidence rather than condemnation and delight rather than drudgery. And when we fall down in sin, we don't wallow in a puddle of guilt. We lift our eyes off ourselves and our failure by taking it straight to our merciful God, and we remember that "if we confess our sins, he is faithful and just to forgive us our sins and to cleanse us from all unrighteousness" (1 John 1:9).

We deal the same way with those long-ago sins that come back to haunt our conscience, whispering that our past choices disqualify us from serving in any meaningful way and from enjoying some of the blessings that come to other believers. We don't give in; instead, we take our conscience straight to God's Word. There we are reminded afresh that, yes, of course our sin disqualifies us! But Christ's qualification has become ours and remains ours as we live our imperfect lives.

If you are weighed down by feelings of condemnation, take a look way back in biblical history at the story of Rahab. If anyone has reason to feel disqualified by past sin, it's an ex-prostitute. That was Rahab, but she put her faith in the Lord and was given a brand-new life, both in this world and the next. She did not allow her former work in the sex trade to define her sense of self or her future. God defined her, and the identity she found in him proved more glorious than she could have imagined. This former prostitute got married and birthed a son in the ancestral line of Jesus himself. How thorough is God's mercy and cleansing work that the DNA of a woman like Rahab could flow through the veins of the perfect Son of God! Moreover, she is held out even today as an example of godly faith (see Heb. 11:31).

Neither our past nor our present defines us. Our sin doesn't define us. Only Christ does, and "there is therefore now no condemnation for those who are in Christ Jesus" (Rom. 8:1).

6

Set Free from Self-Victimization

Bibi Aesha was forced into marriage with a Taliban fighter at age twelve. She endured six years of abuse before managing to escape, only to be caught and ultimately returned to her abusive husband. He punished her by cutting off her nose and ears and leaving her to die on a mountain. Aesha survived, and even though she has a new life in the United States, and a surgically reconstructed face, the abuse she suffered in Afghanistan will impact the rest of her life.[23] Aesha is a victim, if there ever was one.

How would you define that term, *victim*? We hear it so frequently today, as it's regularly applied to anyone who has experienced any kind of suffering in any sort of circumstance. But an indiscriminate application of the term is ultimately harmful because it skews our understanding of what categorizes real victimization. "It's all relative," some would argue, and to a degree that's true. Yet we take it too far. Doesn't it seem a bit absurd to claim someone is suffering because she has a hangnail? "My friend is the victim of a hangnail," or, "My friend is a hangnail survivor"—*seriously?*

A true victim is someone solely at the mercy of her abusers. Children trapped in abusive homes are victims. Women isolated under the tight rein of Sharia law are victims. Parents who lose a child to a drunk driver are victims. True victims are powerless to stop abuse or change their circumstances. And since that's true, we harm more than help when we attach the term *victim*—that identity—to those who are simply suffering the consequences of their own bad choices or those whose sensibilities have been offended by opposing viewpoints.

To flip all that around, in another sense we are all victims. Every one of us is a victim of the ultimate abuser—sin. Left to ourselves, we are powerless against it because, like children trapped in abusive homes, we are born into it. Fueled by Satan, sin tricks, traps, manipulates, and demands to be obeyed, and when we give in, we suffer all the more, and our attempts to escape never work. We need to be rescued not only by someone who can shield us from sin but from someone who can destroy it and the Devil too. That's Jesus, and it's what he came to do. Once in Christ, even though we are harassed by sin, we are its helpless victims no longer. Unless we choose to be.

Dig

Kylie grew up in the home of parents whose lives were embedded in a strict fundamentalist church in which the pastor's word was authoritative, not only over spiritual matters but over work and family life as well. When it came to child raising, he determined good behavior from bad and dictated both reward and punishment. Parents were required to discipline children for joylessness, a look of defiance in the eyes, and reluctance to tend the church grounds every day after school. Discipline for such infractions typically involved severe beatings, which the pastor ordered parents to carry out and then report to him afterward. Needless to say, Kylie's childhood was characterized by fear. And Kylie was most definitely a victim.

Despite her troubling childhood, Kylie has a good relationship with her parents now, three decades later. Shortly after Kylie left home at eighteen, her parents grew disillusioned with the pastor and left the church, and they asked for Kylie's forgiveness, expressing great remorse for the abuse she experienced. Today Kylie attends a sound church. She is married to a kind and gentle man and devotes personal time and resources to a local charity for the homeless. Even so, Kylie doesn't identify first and foremost as a Christian, a wife, or a helper. She defines herself as a victim. Her past overshadows her present.

Living the Past in the Present

Her story isn't uncommon. And it's easy to understand how the trauma of severe abuse can come to define a victim's life. How glorious, then, that when we are united by faith to Christ, he frees us from the past and gives us a whole new identity. "If anyone is in Christ, he is a new creation," Paul writes. "The old has passed away; behold, the new has come" (2 Cor. 5:17). All that has shaped and defined us in the past is over and done with. So if this is true, if the gospel fundamentally disentangles us from the clutches of past trauma, why does Kylie still identify more with her past than with her present and future blessings?

Some of why is simply the reality of life in our fallen world. Kylie does have a brand-new identity in Christ, and therefore the old truly has passed away, but she, like each of us, has been shaped by the totality of all her experiences, both good and bad. As a result, the outworking of her new identity in Christ is a process, one that's likely to unfold to her slowly over months or even years. As of today, Kylie's childhood trauma has always been so much a part of her personal identity that she doesn't know who she is apart from it, so the idea of losing the old identity feels threatening.

I recall her panicked outrage after we attended a lecture in which an older woman shared her own story of childhood abuse. Kylie fumed all the way home, saying, "She thinks she suffered? That's nothing compared to what I went through." Kylie could feel no compassion for this fellow sufferer because, in Kylie's mind, the other woman's suffering seemed somehow to diminish her own. And fueling her outrage was a bit of jealousy, because, unlike Kylie, the lecturer was "compensated" for her suffering by a public platform and crowds of sympathizers. Kylie doesn't yet see that who she is in Christ and what she has in her union with him is so much better.

Retaining her victim identity also helps Kylie justify her anger. Certainly anger at injustice and abuse is a natural reaction, and there is a righteous anger that seeks justice for the oppressed and grieves when evil causes horrific suffering, disfigures creation, and veils God's glory. But Kylie's anger is aimed at God himself. She cannot understand how a good God could have allowed such horror to occur. It's this kind of anger that's always simmering just below her pleasant demeanor and careful words, and it shows on her face more than she realizes. To her way of thinking, God let her down. He failed to protect her, and now he owes her. Part of the problem here is that Kylie hasn't yet grasped the nature of sin—not only the sin of those who harmed her but her own as well. Sin is rightly understood only when it's held up against the holy, righteous nature of God. As Kylie grows in her knowledge of God, she will come to understand that God owes nothing to anyone, and that any good we receive (or bad we avoid) is a gift of God's mercy.

Because Kylie's sense of identity is rooted in the trauma of her early years, she unwittingly short-circuits her present-day life and relationships. Were you to ask her about her many job changes, she'd tell you about micromanager bosses and excessive demands on her time. If you were to ask her about the list of lost friendships, you'd hear about bad listeners and selfish takers. Kylie doesn't see that her unresolved anger and unwillingness to let go of the past rob her of motivation to take on the responsibilities of adulthood and lead her to demand coddling and endless sympathy from friendships that inevitably end.

Discern

As I write, the national news is dominated by yet another school shooting, but the focus of the news isn't the individuals who lost their lives; it's the analysis of why the shooter went on a killing spree. Aside from the arguments for and against gun control, there's all the debate about mental illness, and thrown in is the scrutiny of the shooter's background. Does the blame lie with the environment in which he was raised? Did he have loving parents? Was he bullied in school? People are desperate to find answers, some quantifiable way to explain the mass killing. Surely someone who could brazenly shoot a multitude of fellow teenagers must be a victim of something or someone. Any answer will do—so long as it isn't sin.

I don't want to emulate certain evangelicals in the public spotlight who attribute every natural disaster to societal corruption, but underneath their often ill-advised words is a kernel of truth—all bad things in this world occur ultimately because of sin. The school shooter didn't kill because he had bad parents or because he was ridiculed by his peers. His evil action wasn't the fault of the FBI or deficient counselors or bad gun laws. Parents and institutions and schools can and should play a part in keeping our children safe, but the shooter killed more than a dozen children for one simple reason—he chose to kill them.

What about Addiction?

The belief that we aren't responsible for our sinful choices but instead are victims of them took deeper hold when twelve-step addiction-recovery programs began to proliferate in our communities and churches. Today there are twelve-step programs for every conceivable addiction. A movement that began with Alcoholics Anonymous (AA) in 1939 now includes Clutterers Anonymous, Emotions Anonymous, Overeaters Anonymous, Sexaholics Anonymous, and Underearners Anonymous. While these well-intended programs have undoubtedly helped tens of thousands to manage their addictive behaviors, the most vital component for real recovery—acknowledgment of sin—is often left out.[24] A primary tenet of the twelve-step philosophy is admitting powerlessness over the addictive substance or behavior, but sin itself isn't mentioned in any of the twelve steps. Instead, participants are required to identify with the controlling behavior: "I'm Carrie, and I'm an alcoholic." As a result, Carrie comes to define herself by her drinking addiction. Combine this with the first of the twelve steps—"We admitted we were powerless over alcohol and that our lives had become unmanageable"—and she comes to see herself as a victim of alcohol. Taken altogether, we can understand why addiction is considered by many to be a disease, but that perspective simply doesn't hold up to biblical scrutiny.

First, illness isn't forbidden in Scripture, but drunkenness is.

Second, the characteristics of addiction identified in twelve-step programs parallel how Scripture describes enslavement to sin. Step 1 of AA states, "We admitted we were powerless over alcohol and that our lives had become unmanageable." God's Word says it this way:

> Who has woe? Who has sorrow?
>> Who has strife? Who has complaining?
> Who has wounds without cause?
>> Who has redness of eyes?
> Those who tarry long over wine;
>> those who go to try mixed wine.
> Do not look at wine when it is red,
>> when it sparkles in the cup
>> and goes down smoothly.
> In the end it bites like a serpent
>> and stings like an adder.
> Your eyes will see strange things,
>> and your heart utter perverse things.
> You will be like one who lies down in the midst of the sea,
>> like one who lies on the top of a mast.
> "They struck me," you will say, "but I was not hurt;
>> they beat me, but I did not feel it.
> When shall I awake?
>> I must have another drink." (Prov. 23:29–35)

Both the AA literature and Scripture set forth the powerlessness that accompanies addiction, but only Scripture reveals its true nature. The book of Proverbs, which contains that vivid description of advanced alcoholism, was written to instruct God's people how to live wisely and avoid folly. The illustration was meant to educate young people on the foolishness of drinking to excess. This was, as we say today, a teaching moment, which is clear from the instruction the author includes: *Do not look* at wine when it is red, when it sparkles in the cup."

According to the apostle Peter, people live in drunkenness because *they want to*:

> The time that is past suffices for doing what the Gentiles *want to do*, living in sensuality, passions, drunkenness, orgies, drinking parties, and lawless idolatry. (1 Pet. 4:3)

Over time, however, a desire to escape the consequences begins to compete with the desire to drink, leaving the drinker feeling trapped—addicted. Peter puts it this way: "Whatever overcomes a person, to that he is enslaved" (2 Pet. 2:19).

A Forward Path

Another belief that can lock us into a victim identity arises not from our own sin but from sins committed against us by others. Many hold that we cannot live well in the present or plan for the future until we have gone back and dealt exhaustively with the pain of the past. Although some counselors are now steering away from this approach, it has prevailed among many for decades now. The result is a vast number of wounded people who believe they cannot function normally unless or until they can go back in time and address what happened. But this, too, runs counter to Scripture, which throughout has a forward trajectory. From Genesis to Revelation, we are shown that life in Christ directs us into the future, not the past, and that Jesus himself established this pattern for us:

> Let us also lay aside every weight, and sin which clings so closely, and let us run with endurance the race that is set before us, looking to Jesus, the founder and perfecter of our faith, who for the joy that was set before him endured the cross, despising the shame, and is seated at the right hand of the throne of God. (Heb. 12:1–2)

Flourish

An enslaving habit or damage done to us by others—whatever the source of our hurt—is never healed by downplaying or ignoring the sin that underlies it. Attempting to remove the very real fact of sin harms rather than helps, and it leaves us increasingly hopeless. And wherever the presence of sin is undermined, a victim mind-set is bound to thrive.

Think back for a minute to Kylie. She understands the gospel basics—that Christ paid for her sins and that she now has a perfect Father in heaven—and this has equipped her to forgive her parents for their role in the abuse she experienced. Even so, Kylie struggles with bitterness because she doesn't grasp that the old Kylie is gone, as is the power of the past that previously defined her. From the moment she was joined by faith to Jesus, a process began in which her earlier sufferings are being transformed by the Spirit into something praiseworthy. As she grows in knowledge of her Savior, she will better understand what her salvation means:

> The Spirit of the Lord God is upon me,
>> because the Lord has anointed me
> to bring good news to the poor;
>> he has sent me to bind up the brokenhearted,
> to proclaim liberty to the captives,
>> and the opening of the prison to those who are bound;
> to proclaim the year of the Lord's favor,
>> and the day of vengeance of our God;
>> to comfort all who mourn;
> to grant to those who mourn in Zion—
>> to give them a beautiful headdress instead of ashes,
> the oil of gladness instead of mourning,
>> the garment of praise instead of a faint spirit;
> that they may be called oaks of righteousness,

the planting of the LORD, that he may be glorified.
(Isa. 61:1–3)

A New Identity

We are all victims of something, but when the trauma caused by life in a fallen world, including our own sin, is allowed to define us, we can't grasp that our identity lies with Christ—that our identity *is* Christ. When we are united by faith to Christ, he becomes our identity, and we can say with Paul, "I have been crucified with Christ. It is no longer I who live, but Christ who lives in me" (Gal. 2:20). So gone forever is the need to stand before a twelve-step group and publicly define ourselves by our besetting sin. "I'm Carrie, and I'm an alcoholic" has become "I'm Carrie, and although I struggle not to drink too much, sooner or later the struggle will end, because I am a daughter of the living God."

We also stay stuck in a victim identity if we believe the counsel that peace and a fruitful life will elude us apart from a thorough sifting through past pain. Such counsel goes against the grain of Scripture, which, as we've noted, directs our focus forward rather than back. Instead, we follow Paul's pattern and heed his counsel:

> Brothers, I do not consider that I have made it my own. But one thing I do: forgetting what lies behind and straining forward to what lies ahead, I press on toward the goal for the prize of the upward call of God in Christ Jesus. Let those of us who are mature think this way, and if in anything you think otherwise, God will reveal that also to you. Only let us hold true to what we have attained. (Phil. 3:13–16)

For those in Christ, we are daily becoming what we already are, and all that lies ahead is glorious.

The Suffering of Jesus

Grasping the magnitude of sin—both ours and others'—is vital to getting unstuck from past trauma and flourishing as disciples. One way to strengthen our understanding of sin is to realize that Jesus himself was a victim of sin, and we are the ones who victimized him. All sin deserves death, and Christ experienced this in full on the cross, but the horrendous death he suffered was for our sin, not his own.

If we miss this, we're likely to become bitter, angry, depressed, discouraged, or downright hopeless. We can flourish instead when we understand that Jesus "did" victimhood for us. When he was scorned, mocked, and rejected by loved ones, he didn't grow bitter. When he faced the anguish of the cross, he didn't sink down in despair. When he grew weary from the endless demands on his time and energy, he didn't insist on personal space. When he saw people he loved suffer from the sins of others he loved, he didn't lash out. Instead he prayed. He sought his heavenly Father. He forgave. He healed. He loved. And he grieved.

A friend recently recounted to me a troubling family incident from her childhood, a time when she witnessed a heated argument between her mother and her father. Anger mounted and heated words heaped up, but my friend was powerless to intervene. Eventually her mother crumpled on the floor in exhausted defeat, crying repeatedly, "I wish I were dead!" It's been years since the incident, but my friend still grieves that day, and she described her feelings as a "deep wound." I was struck by that, how sin and its effects wound not just the sinners involved but those who witness the sin as well. Likely we've all received such wounds, and it is perhaps a taste of what Jesus experienced. And surely it's a part of why the Holy Spirit is grieved by our sin (Eph. 4:30).

No matter what we've suffered, it is less than the suffering of our Savior:

> Surely he has borne our griefs
>> and carried our sorrows;
> yet we esteemed him stricken,
>> smitten by God, and afflicted.
> But he was pierced for our transgressions;
>> he was crushed for our iniquities;
> upon him was the chastisement that brought us peace,
>> and with his wounds we are healed. (Isa. 53:4–5)

Letting go of a victim identity isn't to deny what's happened to us. Victimization is very real, and the scars remain. But they can be just that—scars. Scar tissue is present, but it's no longer a wound that needs constant attention. We learn to live with it, and often we find that it becomes a testimony to God's faithfulness. The same can be true of our sin scars. And no matter what we've suffered, the best is still to come.

> I saw the holy city, new Jerusalem, coming down out of heaven from God, prepared as a bride adorned for her husband. And I heard a loud voice from the throne saying, "Behold, the dwelling place of God is with man. He will dwell with them, and they will be his people, and God himself will be with them as their God. He will wipe away every tear from their eyes, and death shall be no more, neither shall there be mourning, nor crying, nor pain anymore, for the former things have passed away."
>
> And he who was seated on the throne said, "Behold, I am making all things new." (Rev. 21:2–5)

Cultivate

A Thirty-Day Study Guide

If you'd like to dig deeper into how the love of Christ frees you from self-focus, this thirty-day study guide is a place to begin. There are five days of study questions for each of the six chapters in *Flourish*.

The study guide has been designed for both individual use and group study. If you decide to proceed on your own, you can devote five days to reading a particular chapter and immersing yourself in the corresponding section of the study guide. Or you might find it more helpful to read the entire chapter before beginning your work. There is no right or wrong way to approach it! Just do what works best for you.

Ideally groups will meet once a week to cover all five days of the study guide for a particular chapter. So, for example, everyone in the group will read chapter 1 and work through the corresponding portion of the study guide individually, and then gather to discuss it. But, even if you do not work on the study guide prior to meeting and instead work through the questions together, reading the chapter before gathering is the way to get the most out of your group time and to foster in-depth discussion.

WEEK 1: SET FREE FROM SELF-CONSCIOUSNESS

Day 1

Take a few minutes to look over your social media footprint.

- What themes emerge from the posts and pictures you've uploaded over the past year?

- As you look back at your Facebook or Instagram selfies, what have you been seeking to communicate about yourself?

- Does the online persona you've projected match the real you? If not, how does it differ?

Day 2

Read Ephesians 2:1–10.

- What do verses 1–3 reveal as the driving force in the hearts and lives of unbelievers?

- How does Paul, the author of this passage, describe the spiritual state of unbelievers?

- How is verse 4 the turning point in the passage?

- Consider all the active verbs in this passage. Which actions are attributed to human beings and which ones to God?

- What attributes of God are revealed in the passage?

- What does this passage reveal about our present spiritual reality as Christians?

- For what purpose have we been saved?

- How does this passage define our identity?

Day 3

Review Sophia's typical day (p. 17) .

- In what ways are you similarly self-conscious in the course of a day? How are you different?

- In what ways is self-consciousness a prison?

- In what areas of your life has the question—*What will people think of me?*—influenced your decisions? How has this impacted you over time?

- Do you attempt to mold your outer person or your family to project a certain image? If so, how, and what do you hope to gain?

- Where do you feel regular pressure to measure up? Where is that pressure coming from?

• How does Proverbs 29:25 speak to the answers you've given here?

Day 4

Read 1 Timothy 4:1–8.

• What do some people do in these later times, or last days, that causes them to turn away from Christianity?

• What false teaching was leading these people away? Why do you think this teaching would make people want to depart from the faith?

• How, in verses 4–5, does Paul refute this false teaching?

• What clue in verse 6 lets us know that the preceding five verses are the context for correctly understanding verses 6–8?

• Considering the context, how would you explain the meaning of verse 8 in your own words?

Day 5

Read Genesis 1:26–31.

• Why is Genesis 1:31 an inadequate foundation on which to build the case for self-esteem?

• How can today's view of the importance of self-esteem fuel our struggle with self-consciousness?

WEEK 2: SET FREE FROM SELF-IMPROVEMENT

Day 6

Read Romans 7:7–25. The apostle is explaining here that God's commandments, called "the law," are good. God's commands become troublesome to us because of the sin in our hearts, which provokes us to dislike God's ways and resist them.

- How does the law enable us to see our sin and what it does to us? See verses 7, 8, and 13.

- How does the entire passage make sense of your own experiences of what Paul describes in verses 15–20?

- What does Romans 7:7–25 teach us about the power of:

  - sin

  - human beings

  - Jesus Christ

- Take time to read Romans 5–8 in a single sitting.

Day 7

- Review Don Matzat's quote on page 33. How do you tend to approach God when it comes to the changes you'd like to make in your life?

- An understanding of Christianity called "moralistic therapeutic deism" has slipped into many of the teachings we receive today (see p. 34). Can you name a specific instance where you've witnessed the thinking that underlies it? How has this misguided understanding impacted your understanding of God and your approach to him?

Day 8

Read 2 Corinthians 12:2–10. The apostle Paul, who refers to himself here in the third person—"I know *a man*"—was given a special experience of God's presence and was shown things that no one else knows.

- On first reading, Paul's talk about boasting might seem a bit confusing or contradictory. On the one hand, it's clear he hates the whole idea of boasting about himself, which is why he refers to himself in the third person. On the other hand, he wants to share his experience. What do you think underlies both his desire to refrain from boasting and his need to mention the experience to his readers? To get a bit deeper into Paul's mind-set here, see also 2 Corinthians 11.

- Why was Paul given a thorn in his flesh, and how does he describe the thorn? Why do you think we aren't told what the actual thorn was?

- What was Paul's initial reaction to his thorn?

- Why did the Lord not remove Paul's thorn, and what do we learn about Christ in the answer he gave to Paul?

- How does the Lord's response to Paul address our thinking about self-improvement?

- Why was Paul able to live contentedly with his thorn and other difficulties?

- Note the differences you see between Paul's response to difficulty and the response of the article author on p. 35.

Day 9

In the Old Testament, Israel is referred to as a vine God planted and tended carefully so that it would produce good fruit to feed all people. But Israel refused to be tended by the divine Gardener, so in time God allowed the vine to grow wild. Read the following passages and note what went wrong:

- Psalm 80:8–18

- Isaiah 5:1–7

- Jeremiah 2:20–22

Read John 15:1–5. How does Israel's failure as a vine get to the heart of what Jesus is saying in John 15:1–5?

- What does it mean to "abide" in Jesus?

- What did Jesus mean when he said that we can do nothing apart from him?

Day 10

What do the following passages teach us about how our thoughts and mind-sets shape our goals and priorities?

- Romans 8:3–6

- Romans 12:1–2

- Ephesians 4:17–24

- Philippians 2:1–7

- Colossians 3:1–4

- James 4:8

- 1 Peter 1:13–15

WEEK 3: SET FREE FROM SELF-ANALYSIS

Day 11

How would you answer the three questions that were posed near the beginning of the chapter? Don't give the "right" answers but the ones that actually drive your life.

- Who am I?

- What do I want?

- What do I feel?

Think back to Sadie and the conversation she had with her friends. Whose advice do you take, and why is their viewpoint influential?

Day 12

Read the apostle Paul's prayers in Ephesians 1:15–23 and 3:14–19.

- Who does Paul pray for?

- What specific requests does Paul make in each prayer?

- How do your prayers tend to differ from Paul's?

- If you were to pray like Paul does here, what sort of answers might you anticipate for yourself and others?

Day 13

Read Exodus 33:18–23, where Moses asks to be shown the glory of God. God's glory is one of his primary attributes. The Hebrew word for *glory* means "heavy" or "weighty."

- How does the Lord's answer to Moses's request reveal the weighty nature of God's glory? List every aspect you can identify in the passage.

- How does this revelation of God's glory differ from how so many think of it today?

Day 14

"Vanity of vanities, says the Preacher, vanity of vanities! All is vanity" (Eccles. 1:2). The author of Ecclesiastes reflects in this book on his life experiences. So much of what he pursued in his youth turned out to be nothing but vanity, or emptiness. What pursuits noted in the following verses proved empty in the long run?

- Ecclesiastes 2:11

- Ecclesiastes 2:15

- Ecclesiastes 2:18–19

- Ecclesiastes 4:4

- Ecclesiastes 4:8

- Ecclesiastes 4:13–16

- Ecclesiastes 5:10

- Ecclesiastes 6:1–2

- Ecclesiastes 6:10–11

- Ecclesiastes 7:5–6

- Ecclesiastes 8:10

- Ecclesiastes 11:10

Day 15

Review the Bible passages (on pp. 52–55) that guide us toward
godly self-analysis.

- Based on these passages, how does godly self-analysis
  differ from the kind we are prone to engage in, both in
  how we go about it and where it leads us?

- Which passages hit home for you, and why?

Cultivate: A Thirty-Day Study Guide

WEEK 4: SET FREE FROM SELF-INDULGENCE

Day 16
Read Luke 17:24–37.

- As Jesus reflects on the history of God's people, he talks about their eating and drinking, marrying, and engaging in commercial activities. Why do you think Jesus paints these activities in a negative light?

- Read Genesis 19:1–29 and explain why Jesus tells the disciples to remember Lot's wife.

- Jesus says in Luke 17:33, "Whoever seeks to preserve his life will lose it, but whoever loses his life will keep it." In light of the history lesson on Sodom that he gives here, what does it mean to preserve your life, and what does it mean to lose it?

- What warning does Jesus issue in Luke 17:33–37? What does this have to do with our theme of self-indulgence?

Day 17

Read James 1:1–8, 12–18.

- Why are we not to despise the trials God allows in our lives?

- What is promised to us in the midst of a trial? What are the conditions for receiving it?

- Failing to trust God in trying times makes us unstable, what James calls "double-minded" (v. 8). What does it mean to be double-minded?

- When you consider your struggles with overindulgence, where might James's teaching in verses 12–15 factor in?

- How is overindulgence an abuse of what we see in verses 16–17? See also John 3:27.

Day 18

Read Ephesians 4:11–16.

- What does the Lord intend to bring about in the gathered body of God's people? List every aspect of spiritual growth you see here.

- How does Paul's teaching here run counter to today's focus on self-care as the means to health and growth?

Day 19

Read Galatians 5:16–24.

- What stark contrast does Paul paint in verse 16, and what reason does he give in verse 17 for the contrast?

- Consider the "works of the flesh" list in verses 19–21 alongside the fruit of the Spirit listed in verses 22–23.

- What makes the first set of works "fleshly"?

- Why do you think people are drawn to the works of the flesh, and what do they produce?

- Why do you think Paul calls the second list "fruit of the Spirit"?

- How is this fruit produced in our lives?

- Considered together, why are works of the flesh rightly categorized as self-indulgent, but not the fruit of the Spirit?

Day 20

Read Matthew 8:18–22.

- What does Jesus's response to the scribe indicate about the sort of heart necessary for discipleship?

- Scripture upholds the importance of caring for family members (see, for example, 1 Tim. 5:8), so we know that Jesus isn't asking the disciple here to dishonor his father. What then does Jesus mean?

- Are you aware of particular indulgences that hold you back from growing up in your faith? If so, why do you cling to them?

- If the prospective cost of following Christ has made you fearful, and this fear routinely fuels quick-fix escapes into overindulgence, how can the following passages aid you?

    - John 10:7–10

    - Ephesians 1:16–18

    - 1 Timothy 6:17

WEEK 5: SET FREE FROM SELF-CONDEMNATION

Day 21

- Do you regularly put yourself down? If so, what beliefs underlie your self-condemning words or thoughts?

Day 22

Read Romans 8:31–39, where Paul summarizes everything he has covered earlier in the letter. Paul asks a series of rhetorical questions as he begins this summary passage. How would you answer each of Paul's questions? Write your answers below.

- "If God is for us, who can be against us?" (v. 31)

- "He who did not spare his own Son but gave him up for us all, how will he not also with him graciously give us all things?" (v. 32)

- "Who shall bring any charge against God's elect?" (v. 33)

- "Who is to condemn?" (v. 34)

- "Who shall separate us from the love of Christ?" (v. 35)

Day 23

How does each of the following passages define our actual status in Christ?

- Isaiah 61:10

- Luke 15:11–24

- 1 Corinthians 6:9–11

- Ephesians 5:25–27

- Titus 3:4–7

- Hebrews 10:19–23

- Revelation 7:13–14

Day 24

Read Luke 7:36–50.

- Whom does Jesus address in this passage, and what is his point?

- Why does the woman in the passage weep?

- What link does Jesus make between love and forgiveness?

- To what does Jesus attribute the woman's salvation?

Day 25

Read 1 John 1:5–10.

- What does it mean to walk in darkness? Conversely, how do we walk in the light?

- What link does John make between walking in light and being cleansed from sin? Knowing that we are saved *by faith alone*, what link can we be sure John is *not* making?

- John says that denying our sinfulness is an indicator that we are self-deceived and unsaved. Why is this true?

- Confessing our sins isn't why we are forgiven—we are forgiven because Christ paid for those sins. So what does John mean when he writes, "If we confess our sins, he is faithful and just to forgive us our sins" (v. 9)? Why is God faithful and just in offering us forgiveness?

WEEK 6: SET FREE FROM SELF-VICTIMIZATION

Day 26

- Write out your own definition of the word *victim*. What experiences or observations have shaped your viewpoint?

Day 27

Read Romans 6:3–19.

- Once we have been baptized into Christ's death and resurrection, how is our relationship to sin fundamentally changed?

- How are we called to act on our faith in order to live out our new reality?

- What is promised to us in verse 14?

- Jot down the specific ways Romans 6:3–19 reveals that our union with Christ renders us no longer helpless victims of besetting sins and addictions.

Day 28

Read Hebrews 11:1–12:2.

- In what ways would the "faith heroes" of Hebrews 11 be classified as victims today? How did they handle their difficulties, and what was the outcome for each?

- What two things are we called to set aside in 12:1, and what are we called to pursue? How can this call free us from living with a victim mentality?

- In what way is Jesus our primary example for how to escape the ways we've been damaged by sin—either our own or someone else's?

Day 29

Scripture shows us that the trajectory of the Christian life is forward rather than backward. Record how this is evidenced in the passages below:

- Psalm 45:10–11

- 1 Corinthians 9:24

- Hebrews 11:8–10

- Philippians 3:12–14, 20

- James 1:12

- 1 John 3:2–3

- Revelation 21:1–4

Day 30

Read Isaiah 53:1–12, which is a prophecy about the coming Messiah and the work he would do.

- Isaiah prophesies how Jesus would be treated. Note all the ways Jesus was victimized, and by whom.

- For what purpose did Jesus become a victim?

- How does Jesus's response to his mistreatment differ from your typical response?

- Why can we say that Jesus "did" victimhood for us?

- How does this passage alter your perspective on your own suffering?

Notes

1. Aliza Latta, "Dear Girl Who Thinks She's Not Enough," November 9, 2017, (in)courage website, accessed February 27, 2018, http://www.in courage.me/2017/11/dear-girl-who-thinks-shes-not-enough.html.
2. Latta, "Dear Girl Who Thinks She's Not Enough."
3. Timothy Keller, *The Freedom of Self-Forgetfulness* (Lancashire, UK: 10 Publishing, 2012), 32.
4. This wording was first put forth by Augustine. For a really helpful explanation of his teaching on sin, including a handy diagram, see "Human Nature in Its Fourfold State," Monergism.com, accessed July 5, 2018, https://www.monergism.com/thethreshold/articles/onsite /four-fold.html.
5. Don Matzat, *Christ Esteem: Where the Search for Self-Esteem Ends* (Eugene, OR: Harvest, 1990), 52.
6. For a quick summary explanation of moralistic therapeutic deism (and a fun diagram!), see Adam Ford, "Moralistic Therapeutic Deism (webcomic)," Adam4d.com, accessed July 5, 2018, http://adam4d.com/mtd/.
7. Lysa TerKeurst, "From Overpowered to Empowered," (in)courage website, accessed January 13, 2017, http://www.incourage.me/2013/05 /from-overpowered-to-empowered.html.
8. TerKeurst, "From Overpowered to Empowered."
9. Owen Strachan, introduction to *Designed for Joy: How the Gospel Impacts Men and Women, Identity and Practice*, ed. Jonathan Parnell and Owen Strachan (Wheaton, IL: Crossway, 2015), 18.
10. Samuel James, "The Hyper-Examined Life Is Not Worth Living in 2017," The Gospel Coalition website, December 30, 2016, accessed January 23, 2018, https://www.thegospelcoalition.org/article/the-hyper-examined -life-is-not-worth-living/.
11. Jennifer Dukes Lee, *The Happiness Dare* (Carol Stream, IL: Tyndale Momentum, 2016), 33–34; emphasis added.

12. Tim Challies, "On Christian Coloring Books and Meaningful Hobbies," Challies.com, February 9, 2017, accessed March 6, 2018, https://www.challies.com/articles/on-christian-coloring-books-and-meaningful-hobbies/.

13. "Life Coach Training Basics" (course description), Wheaton College website, accessed March 6, 2018, https://www.prisoninstitute.com/life-coach-training.

14. Laurie Beth Jones, *Jesus Life Coach: Learn from the Best* (Nashville, TN: Thomas Nelson, 2004), xv, 3.

15. Marshall Segal, "The Insanity of Self-Care," Desiring God website, March 14, 2016, accessed February 3, 2018, https://www.desiringgod.org/articles/the-insanity-of-self-care.

16. Ray S. Anderson, back cover of *Self-Care: A Theology of Personal Empowerment and Spiritual Healing* (Eugene, OR: Wipf & Stock, 2010). See https://www.amazon.com/Self-Care-Theology-Empowerment-Spiritual-Collection/dp/1610970594.

17. Dee Eastman and April O'Neil, "Why the Daniel Plan Works," *The Daniel Plan* website, January 13, 2013, accessed March 6, 2018, http://www.danielplan.com/blogs/dp/why-the-daniel-plan-works/.

18. *ESV Study Bible* (Wheaton, IL: Crossway, 2008), Dan. 1:8–16 note.

19. Moriah Nelson, "Freedom in Forgiveness," (in)courage website, September 30, 2014, accessed February 16, 2018, http://www.incourage.me/2014/09/freedom-in-forgiveness.html.

20. Nelson, "Freedom in Forgiveness."

21. John MacArthur, *The Vanishing Conscience* (Dallas, TX: Word, 1994), 44.

22. If you want to learn more about training your conscience, a good resource is Andrew David Naselli and J. D. Crowley, *Conscience: What It Is, How to Train It, and Loving Those Who Differ* (Wheaton, IL: Crossway, 2016).

23. Jessica Ravitz, "Saving Aesha," CNN website, accessed February 21, 2018, http://www.cnn.com/interactive/2012/05/world/saving.aesha/?hpt=hp_c2.

24. Celebrate Recovery was established in 1991 in an effort to bring a more biblical emphasis to the twelve-step recovery process. See the Celebrate Recovery website, accessed February 22, 2018, http://www.celebraterecovery.com/.

General Index

Scripture Index

Also Available from Lydia Brownback

"Read and experience how God's wisdom is eloquent and transcendent while being concrete and practical at the same time."

PAUL DAVID TRIPP, President, Paul Tripp Ministries; author,
New Morning Mercies

"In *A Woman's Wisdom*, we're invited to saturate ourselves in the source of true wisdom—the Scriptures—where we find what we need for living in a world full of distractions, decisions, dilemmas, disappointments, and delights."

NANCY GUTHRIE, Bible teacher; author, Seeing Jesus in the
Old Testament Bible study series

For more information, visit **crossway.org**.

Also Available from Lydia Brownback

"A remarkable book with a culturally timely message!"

JONI EARECKSON TADA, Founder and CEO, Joni and Friends
International Disability Center

"I don't think I've ever read anything on loneliness that seemed to get to the heart of it, or applied any real wisdom to it until *Finding God in My Loneliness.*"

NANCY GUTHRIE, author, *Even Better than Eden: Nine Ways the Bible's Story Changes Everything about Your Story*

For more information, visit **crossway.org**.